D1623812

Presented to:

Stefanie Jacob '97

From:

Dorothy Cebula, Ph.D.

Date:

_Dec. 21, 1997 · With warmest
regards_

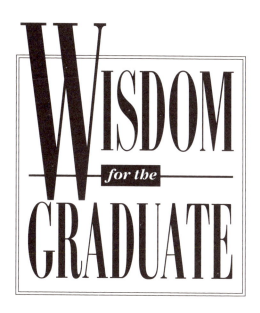

WISDOM
for the
GRADUATE

Larry
Richards

ZondervanPublishingHouse
Grand Rapids, Michigan

A Division of HarperCollins*Publishers*

WISDOM FOR THE GRADUATE

Copyright © 1988 by Lawrence O. Richards
This book is excerpted from
The Believer's Guidebook,
Copyright © 1983 by Lawrence O. Richards

Requests for information should be addressed to:
Zondervan Publishing House
Grand Rapids, Michigan 49530

Library of Congress Cataloging in Publication Data

Richards, Larry, 1931–
  Wisdom for the graduate / Larry Richards.
    p. cm.
    1. Students—Religious life. 2. Students—Conduct of life.
I. Title.
BV4531.2.R456   1988
248.8'3–dc19   87-34527
                                                           CIP

ISBN 0-310-39710-3

Edited by Martha Manikas-Foster and Shelley Hudson
Interior design by Martha Manikas-Foster
Cover design by Jim Connelly

Printed in the United States of America

96 97 98 99 / DH / 6 5 4 3

This edition is printed on acid-free paper and meets the American National Standards Institute Z39.48 standard.

CONTENTS

INTRODUCTION

Graduation. Commencement. The marking of one stage of life completed and the anticipation of another bursting forth.

This graduation represents a passage for you. And as you go through the changes that must accompany this passage, you will look for guides through the unfamiliar territory.

Larry Richards asks to be one of those guides. In *Wisdom for the Graduate,* he draws from his experience as a Christian educator, Bible teacher, and author, to compile an alphabetical listing of topics important to graduates. These are bits of wisdom you will find yourself referring to in the months and even the years after the commencement ceremony is over and the mortarboard tucked away.

The Editor

ACHIEVEMENT

We are motivated by achievement: in education, in professions, in hobbies. Psychologists have come to believe that achievement is one of our basic motivations. We have a drive to accomplish by the exercise of our ability and efforts. Some dislike this notion. It seems to smack of self-effort—something they identify as a basic sin. But God seems to approve of achievement. The Bible even suggests that the ability to achieve is one of God's gifts to us.

ADULT

Is a person a full-fledged adult at 21—the old voting age? Or at 19? Or maybe at 16, when drivers' licenses are passed out? Or at 18, when a person can join the army!

There is no confusion about adulthood and maturity in the Bible, however. It doesn't connect adulthood with a specific age, and it certainly doesn't connect maturity with society's headlong dash into silly sins. The Bible views adulthood as ethical maturity. The idea of adulthood is related to a Greek word that means reaching a goal or in being perfected. John uses the same word in speaking of love: maturity is seen in a love that is an expression of obedience to God (1 John 2:5) and of a deep caring for others (4:12). The Bible also has this to say about maturity, "In regard to evil be infants, but in your thinking be adults" (1 Cor. 14:20).

ALIENATION

Whenever we move from one phase of our lives into another, it's not unusual to feel isolated and cut off. Some social scientists have called our age the age of alienation. In some cases, we become indifferent to or suspicious of others and tend to turn away. This kind of behavior can only aggravate our feelings of isolation, for alienation only deepens when we are alone. Soon life itself can seem unreal and vague. If you've ever felt the loneliness and uncertainty of alienation, you know how important it is to find your way back. Back to reality. And back to relationships.

The New Testament speaks of about three different kinds of alienation. The first is alienation from God. Remember when you weren't a Christian? Here's how Colossians describes how we were: "Once you were alienated from God and were enemies in your minds because of your evil behavior" (1:21).

This kind of alienation takes the form of suspicion and hostility. There's a nagging sense of guilt associated with sin that makes humanity look hesitantly over one shoulder, sure that God can't be there but always afraid that He is. God doesn't seem real. But the very idea that He might be is uncomfortable and impels us to turn away.

God has dealt decisively with this kind of alienation through Christ. Colossians 1:22 tells us, "Now he
has reconciled you by Christ's physical body through
death to present you holy in his sight, without blemish
and free from accusation." With the good news of the
gospel, we discover we have nothing to fear. God is not
our accuser! Jesus has dealt with our sin and offers us
the bright robes of His holiness. We're free to turn back
to the God from whom we fled, amazed to learn He's
followed us all these years only that He might be our
Friend.

The second kind of alienation the New Testament
speaks of is from other human beings. Even in the early
church there were people eager to create splinter
groups, to sow suspicion and fear. "Those people are
jealous to win you over," Paul warns the Galatians,
"but for no good. What they want is to alienate you
from us, so that you may be zealous for them" (Gal.
4:17).

Alienation is a great danger for us, for when we
build our barriers and plug our ears, we cut ourselves
off from the vital, living body of which the New
Testament says we are a part. The more we cut
ourselves off from others the more lonely and isolated
we feel. We will stop growing; it is within the warm
network of intimate relationships that God nurtures us.
And the whole body of Christ will be affected: "Joined
and held together by every supporting ligament," the
whole body "grows and builds itself up in love, as each
part does its work" (Eph. 4:16).

There are some very practical steps we can take to

break out of our isolation and gradually rebuild trust in and love for other believers.

(1) Consciously identify with God's people. There will be differences you'll notice. But remember as a Christian you are a child of God. Others who confess Christ are your brothers and sisters. Consciously identifying yourself as a member of a family is a first basic step.

(2) Listen to others and try to understand how they think and feel. Don't be judgmental, but accepting. Remind yourself that you don't have to agree with others to care about them.

(3) Take the risk of communicating. Let others know what you think and how you feel. There's no security in wearing a false face. It will only cut us off, deepening our alienation. When we are ourselves with others and find they accept us, we come to realize we're not alone.

For a person who feels alienated, steps like these aren't easy. But they needn't be rushed. You can join a group of believers and sit quietly among them as long as you wish. You can listen to others and develop a habit of praying for them as you sense their needs and concerns. And then you can begin gradually to share your own thoughts and feelings and needs.

The third kind of alienation in the New Testament might be called alienation from the source of power. The verse that mentions this is probably one of the most misunderstood in Scripture. "You who are trying to be justified by law have been alienated from Christ. You have fallen away from grace" (Gal. 5:4). In this great letter Paul is writing of a dilemma experi-

enced by many Christians today. Having come to
Christ, we're eager to please Him and are desperate to
find our way out of the barrenness of an empty life into
the rich fullness of a life in Christ. But like some of the
Christians in Paul's day we try to find that new life by
adopting the strict regulations in the Old Testament. In
turning back to the Law, we lose sight of Jesus and can
become indifferent to Him. We, like the Galatians, fail
to realize that "the only thing that counts is faith
expressing itself through love" (Gal. 5:6).

Wherever we turn in Scripture we make a
common discovery about alienation. It is emptiness: a
loneliness that exists within men and women as an
aching void. For the lost, the promise of Scripture is
that Jesus will fill the void. For us, the promise is that
when we reach out to others they become no longer
strangers but family.

ANXIETY

Picture yourself applying for a new job. Or
taking a test that might affect the rest of your life. Or
waiting, for the first time in your life, in an unemploy-
ment line. Or going to the dentist for an abscessed
tooth. Or waiting in a doctor's office for a diagnosis.
We all know the feelings that can come at times like
these. We all experience anxiety.

Psychologists have defined anxiety as a feeling of
apprehension, cued by a threat to something we hold

essential. Normal anxiety is (1) an appropriate reaction (2) to an objective threat (3) which is relieved when the objective situation changes. The way to handle normal anxiety is to cope—to admit our feelings, then face the situation and deal with it. When David was anxious this is what he told God, "When I am afraid, I will trust in you" (Psalm 56:3). Trust did not drive out his fear. But fear gave David an opportunity to exercise trust. When we face our anxieties with trust in God, we will be able to cope.

At times people respond to anxiety in destructive rather than constructive ways. Someone may run out of a business's office when the receptionist says, "Your interview is next." Or someone else's mind goes blank when the test is handed out, even though the material has been thoroughly studied. While trust won't remove our fears, confidence in God's presence will enable us to meet rather than flee from or repress our fears.

For some people anxiety is a constant companion. Their anxiety isn't linked to a specific objective threat but has become a constant unease. We've all known anxious people, always tense and afraid even when there seems to be no cause. There are anxious Christians too. But the believer has a tremendous advantage when it comes to dealing with anxiety. Even when a believer cannot locate an objective cause for anxiety, there is something he or she can do. That is to consciously relate to a God who holds us securely in His Hand.

The psalmist shared a personal experience with anxiety in the words of Psalm 94:18, 19. "When I said 'My foot is slipping,' your love, O LORD, supported

me. When anxiety was great within me, your consola-
tion brought joy to my soul." Despite feelings of
helplessness he was anchored in the supportive love of
God.

The New Testament gives this same prescription
for dealing with both normal and neurotic anxiety. We
are to recognize and express our feelings of anxiety to
God. "Cast all your anxiety on him," Peter says,
"because he cares for you" (1 Peter 5:7). Paul expands
on Peter's words and adds a promise. "Do not be
anxious about anything, but in everything, by prayer
and petition, with thanksgiving, present your requests
to God. And the peace of God, which transcends all
understanding, will guard your heart and your minds in
Christ Jesus" (Phil. 4:6, 7).

AUTHORITY

There's hardly a more dangerous word in our
vocabulary. In the world it implies the right to control.
In Christ "authority" must be understood as the right
to influence.

The reason for the difference is that authority has
a different purpose in each setting. The world is
concerned about how others behave, and so authority is
meant to control behavior. Christ is concerned about
inner transformation and maturity, so authority has to
do with helping others grow.

Jesus describes the secular approach to authority

in Matthew 20:24–25. He pictures an authority that
relies on position (that is, people "over" other people)
and on power. This kind of authority forces others to
conform to certain demands. While such authority wins
compliance, it often creates resentment. Position and
power are ineffective when it comes to winning an
eager and willing response from people.

So when Jesus was describing the secular approach to the disciples, he told them bluntly, "Not so
with you" (Matt. 20:26). He wanted to teach them a
different kind of authority, and the model He used was,
strangely enough, a servant. "Whoever wants to
become great among you," he said, "must be a
servant." It is in the servant that we discover an
authority unknown in the world.

Several passages in Scripture give more detail
about the kind of authority Jesus sketched for the
disciples. We see that it is not exercised from a position
above others but "among" them (20:26, cf. Matt. 23:8–
11). Rather than demanding others to act a certain way,
this authority calls for providing an example. Rather
than forcing others to conform, this authority trusts a
working of God within other people. When Paul wrote
about spiritual authority to the Corinthians, he pointed
out that its goal is to build others up. In this context the
one with authority will teach and urge, not demand
(2 Cor. 8:8, 9; 9:7).

Living in our society, it's difficult to visualize
how servant authority works. We live in a world where
those in authority tell, require, direct, praise, reward,
or fire. The idea of servant authority seems weak in

comparison. And yet because it has the power to transform people it is the most potent of all.

What are basic principles for exercising spiritual authority? (1) Build a close personal relationship with others. Do not try to lead or to relate from a position "above" or over them. (2) Be a good model or example. Demonstrate your own personal commitment to what you encourage others to do. (3) Teach. Communicate as clearly as possible the beliefs and values that guide your own actions. (4) Continue to relate, to model, and to teach faithfully, even when response seems to come slowly. Trust God to work in others' lives, and pray that He will motivate and discipline them.

There is a place for the secular form of authority in the world. We would hardly try to replace the military chain-of-command authority with servant authority. But servant authority is appropriate in the church, and it is effective only because of the presence and power of the Holy Spirit in believers. And yet in every situation we will need to heed Jesus' warning about the world's authority: "Not so with you." For us, God has a far better and more powerful way.

BEAUTY

Have you ever yearned to be really beautiful? Then think about this. As a nineteenth-century woman you would have struggled to display overly plump breasts and buttocks; as a man nothing less than an imposingly big belly would have done. Of course, today men struggle to keep trim, and women starve themselves in order to imitate the emaciated models our society so admires. Depending on your era and nationality, you might have scarred your face, enlarged your lips and ear lobes, squeezed into an hour-glass corset, added mud or paints or powders to your face, and worn scents galore. What a strange thing, this search for beauty. And how deceptive.

Peter writes to believers about beauty. "Your beauty should not come from outward adornment, such as braided hair and the wearing of gold jewelry and fine clothes. Instead, it should be that of your inner self, the unfading beauty of a gentle and quiet spirit, which is of great worth in God's sight. For this is the way the holy women of the past who put their hope in God used to make themselves beautiful" (1 Peter 3:3–5).

It's not wrong for a Christian to be in style. But we must realize that true beauty is an inner beauty. If "beauty" becomes competition then we need to follow the advice Paul gave to some who made church just another dress-up affair: "I also want women to dress modestly, with decency and propriety, not with braided hair or gold or pearls or expensive clothes, but with good deeds, appropriate for women who profess to worship God" (1 Tim. 2:9, 10).

BECOMING

To understand "becoming" we need to learn an unusual rule of evidence that has to do with what is seen and what is unseen.

Paul is the one who teaches this principle to the young believers at Corinth. When he looked at their lives he saw how they were divided over doctrine; parties had formed around favorite teachers; they had a casual attitude toward sexual immorality; and believers accused each other of fraud. No wonder he called these people worldly, "acting like mere men" (1 Cor. 3:3).

It would have been fairly easy for Paul to give up on them or to let them know how hopeless they were. But he didn't. He remained optimistic and even told them "I have great confidence in you" (2 Cor. 7:4). "We fix our eyes not on what is seen, but on what is unseen," Paul explained. "What is seen is temporary, but what is unseen is eternal" (2 Cor. 4:18). The things he saw in the Corinthians could and would change, so they did not count. What Paul was concerned about was "what is in the heart" (2 Cor. 5:12). He was convinced that transformation is brought about by the compelling love of Christ (5:14).

In Christ we are each a "new creation; the old has gone, the new has come" (2 Cor. 5:17). Renewed within, we can count on God's own incomparable power, and we can know that we will "become the righteousness of God" (2 Cor. 5:21). So the evidence that counts is not what we see *now*. The evidence that counts is hidden from our view.

The New Testament describes the impact of Jesus in our lives in these words: we "are being transformed into his likeness with ever-increasing glory, which comes from the Lord, who is the Spirit" (2 Cor. 3:18). God is at work. The process is taking place. We are not what we are. We are what we are becoming.

BUDGETING

A budget is a spending plan, designed to help you set goals and allocate your money accordingly. I've gotten along without a family budget for twenty-six years. For one simple reason. As soon as any money has come in, it's rushed out again. Why worry about a budget when there's nothing extra anyway?

The experts tell me I've been foolish. If I had analyzed my costs, they say, I'd probably be a lot better off by now. At least I'd have a better handle on my spending patterns, and I would know for sure how I use what money I do have. Keeping a budget does let me *know* what's going on with my money. I'm quite sure that one meaning of that "self-control" the New Testament sets such store by involves getting control of the use of my money. "Where your treasure is," Jesus said, "there will your heart be also." Is it possible that at times I've been the victim of a straying heart and never even realized it? It might be good to know.

CAREERS

For most of us, life is oriented around our work. Most of our time and effort are invested in our job. Work provides income and a sense of personal achievement, so our career is important in many ways.

For many people these days life will hold more than one career. Technological changes have forced many changes in lifestyle, opening undreamed-of work opportunities and shutting down old, familiar ones. What we know about careers and how to choose them can help those just beginning in the work world.

Geography. Certain states will continue population growth, which will create job opportunities. A person willing to locate in one of the growth areas may have a better chance finding a job he or she wants. The best states? Statistics suggest Idaho, Nevada, Utah, Arizona, Colorado, Alaska, Florida, and Hawaii. These are closely followed by Wyoming, New Mexico, Texas, Georgia, North and South Carolina, and Virginia. The first group of states can expect over 30% growth, a growth that began in 1975 and is expected to end about 1990. The second group of states can expect growth between 20% and 29%.

Occupations. Studies of trends in occupations also suggest that certain fields offer better opportunities than others. For instance, you're likely to be disappointed if you'd planned to become a lawyer, a doctor, an airline pilot, or a file clerk. On the other hand, things are looking up for various medical aides and assistants, scientists, engineers, secretaries, and computer related workers. In blue collar areas things look good for electricians, plumbers, mechanics, and repairmen.

You and a career. It's just as important to evaluate your own personality and goals when thinking of a career as it is to evaluate the job market. What do career counselors suggest a person should evaluate?

• Will you be more comfortable with routine work or work that calls for imagination and ingenuity? The first alternative provides pattern and security. The second brings risk of failure and insecurity.

• Will you be more comfortable in a large or small organization? The first tends to be impersonal and calls for working through bureaucratic channels. An individual seldom sees the immediate impact of his or her contribution and has proportionately smaller influence. In the small organization you work through personal contact and see the impact of your decisions quickly.

• Will you be more comfortable working up from the bottom or starting near the top, perhaps as a "management trainee"? Near the bottom you make fewer serious mistakes, but it takes longer to advance. Near the top you're vulnerable to jealousy and have opportunities to make glaring errors.

• Will you be most comfortable as a specialist or generalist? The specialist is trained in a technical or professional field and is an expert in one clearly defined area. The generalist usually is in management, working with people, with planning, and with the coordination of others' efforts.

Training. Some occupations call for in-service training or technical schools, and others require college.

If you plan on college without graduate school, most counselors today suggest focusing on courses that quickly equip you for a career. Many colleges now offer special evening training courses for older people who want to change careers. And of course skills gained in one field may well transfer to a new field. It's wise to have some notion of your area of interest and your temperament before you enroll in training programs.

The Christian dimension. While opportunity and personal temperament will play a valid role in the search for a career, the Christian adds another consideration: ministry. In a very real way, every occupation should be viewed as ministry. Work not only pays our way through life and brings personal satisfaction, it also provides an avenue of service to others.

Ministry can take many forms. The builder who creates homes where families will live, the travel agent who helps plan vacations, and the nurse who gives patients emotional support as well as medicine are all ministries as much as preaching or the counseling of a pastor.

We should be aware of how our jobs are a ministry. For one builder I know, satisfaction comes with providing, at a fair price, quality homes, which are designed to enrich life. Others I know must be in direct touch with people for them to have the sense that their work is a ministry.

This, then, is something to consider in deciding on a career. What is my vision of ministry? What can I do to best serve others through my work? Whatever you choose, you can know that work *is* serving others, so "whatever you do, whether in word or deed, do it all in the name of the Lord Jesus, giving thanks to God the Father through him" (Col. 3:17).

CARING

A recent, well-known experiment shows how important caring is. A number of students at a theological seminary were sent on an errand along a route where they would pass a person who appeared to be ill. Some were going to preach a sermon on the Good Samaritan. Others were simply carrying a message for a professor. It didn't seem to make much difference whether a student's thoughts were on the Good Samaritan or the prof. Some stopped to help. Others did not.

But the insight into caring came when the experimenters noted *how* different students helped. Some helped and then went on their way when the man feigning illness claimed to be better. Others simply would not let him go. They insisted on buying him coffee or a coke or hovered beside him even when he insisted he was able to go on alone. The experimenters reached this conclusion: some helped out of concern for the man and when he was better, released him. But some helped because they needed to be helpers! They would not let him go because their own psychological needs were being met by another person depending on them.

It's important for Christians to care. But Christian caring focuses on others in need, on helping them get back on their feet. It is *not* having our own needs met, even though that may well be a consequence of caring.

CHOICES

Making choices helps a person feel free and competent, particularly when the kinds of choices are between positive alternatives. God entrusts us with the freedom to choose. He invites us to look around and see a number of ways we can invest our time and energy to serve Him and enrich others' lives. Then we can evaluate, pray, and make our own choice from an array of alternatives of how to do good.

CHURCH

Finding a local church can be frustrating because there are usually several in a community to choose from. How do we decide?

Now some of us have been brought up in a particular tradition and just naturally head for the representative of our denomination. Others visit around, to look and listen. Does the doctrinal statement express our persuasion? Do we like the preacher? Is there an active group for singles? A good choir we might join? We check down our shopping list, look carefully at what each congregation may have to offer, and then make our decision.

I agree that these concerns are important. But I wonder if they are as all-important as we sometimes make them. The Bible's picture of the church may suggest other things we need to evaluate as well.

The church in Scripture. "Church" is a Greek word (*ekklēsia*) used for centuries before the Christian era to mean an assembly of people. In the sense of "church" it is used only in the epistles, to identify fellowships that came into being after the resurrection of Jesus. There this "church" is always viewed as a community of believers: as men and women who have responded to God's call to faith in Jesus and who formed ranks as a witness to the world. There's no hint of denominations in the Bible. The church is limited geographically: it is the "church at Corinth" or the "church that meets in your home." God's people are all one company, linked in solidarity with all other believers.

There are two dominating word pictures in the Bible portraying this new assembly. The church is said to be a body. And the church is said to be a family.

• The body represents a living organism, with Jesus Himself as Head. This word picture speaks of an organic relationship between the individual believer and Jesus, and between believer and believer. This vision of the church as a body emphasizes the fact that, like parts of a physical body, each member in the spiritual body of Christ has a distinctive function. This emphasis is found in these passages: Romans 12; 1 Corinthians 12; Ephesians 4. In them we see that each person is placed by God within the body, and each is given special enablement by the Holy Spirit to fulfill his role there "for the common good" (1 Cor. 12:7). Each Christian is to use his or her gift to minister to others. Through the active ministry of each person in the body, other individuals and the whole congregation grow toward Christian maturity. And new members are drawn to Jesus and joined to the living church.

This New Testament picture emphasizes the priesthood of all believers and insists that we Christians understand ourselves as persons called to minister to and serve each other. "Church" is not God's people, seated well-dressed in tidy rows, but "church" is God's people ministering and interacting. In the few New Testament portraits we have of the church gathering for meetings people are doing different things: speaking, sharing, offering a teaching, leading in prayer, suggesting a song, and encouraging one another (cf. 1 Cor. 14:26–33; Heb. 10:23–25).

• The New Testament constantly reflects the family character of the church. The family affirms an intimate relationship between believers, with God Himself the Father (cf. Eph. 3:14–19). Believers are called brothers and sisters and are spoken of in other family terms (cf. 1 Thess. 2:7–13; 1 Tim. 5:1, 2). Again and again, each apostle urges Christians to love one another with brotherly love, to accept and encourage each other, to share joy as well as tears, to rebuke each other when necessary, and to forgive.

Clues to a vital local church. With these New Testament images of the church in mind, what are some of the things we should desire in a local congregation?

• Loving, intimate relationships. Try to get a sense of what characterizes relationships of the people in this congregation. Are the people warm—not just to you, but with each other? When you ask a person about others, like "that couple over there," what kinds of things do they share? Check out the church bulletin too. Are the activities listed formal meetings or agency activities? Or do groups meet for sharing, prayer, and Bible study?

• Caring for persons. This is another critical aspect of loving. You can tell a lot just by visiting a Sunday morning service. Does the teaching reflect a personal touch? Are personal illustrations used? Is the Bible related to real-life issues in a positive, encouraging way? Do announcements reflect involvement in the lives and concerns of people in the congregation?

• Ministering by all. This is a vital consideration, reflecting as it does the basic body teaching of the New Testament. Is most of the congregation passive, while the hired staff does the work of ministry? When you talk with people, do they seem to have a sense of ministry, a feeling of excitement about what God is doing in the lives of others? One good indication is the role of the elders/deacons of the congregation. Are they seen as respected spiritual leaders? Or are they viewed more as a board that meets to vote on the business of the church?

• Testifying to the world. Jesus was quite clear when He taught that a loving fellowship will make it plain to the world that they are His disciples (John 13:35). Check the perception of people in the community who do not go to that church. How are the members viewed? As distant and "stand-offish" or warm and caring?

Making your choice. When it comes to choosing a local church, you and I want to look at the more obvious things, like the doctrinal statement and agencies. But we also want to look beneath the surface, to see the inner dynamics of the people as they live together. Sometimes we'll find that ideal church we dream of. Too often no congregation in our area approaches the ideal. What do we do then?

Earlier I wrote about looking carefully "at what each congregation may have to offer." But should our concern be with what the congregation can offer *us,* or what we can offer it? Is "church" just a social service agency, and we go to the one that offers the most services? Or is "church" really the people of God, and we join them because we are called by God to be with our brothers and sisters, to love and to serve them? What I'm suggesting is that perhaps the most important thing to do in selecting a local church is to pray and seek God's leading to that group of people whom God most wants *us* to serve.

In the final analysis, what is really exciting is to realize that the church truly *is* people. That even if people aren't loving now, we can love them. And that if people aren't ministering to others now, we can be God's servant by ministering to them. By being a

loving, caring, and serving person, we may find that
He has a ministry for us in a congregation that is far
from perfect, but which still is made up of people
whom He—and we—can love.

COLLEGE

Many high school graduates today are expected to
go on to college. They may be uncertain about which
college to attend and which major area of study to
pursue. But for most parents and kids, college is the
thing to do. After all, many believe a degree is a
passport to getting ahead financially in today's world.

Why not to go to college. Before we join the
herd going off to college, we might consider first
whether or not college might be a waste of our time
and money. Consider these facts. Professors admit that
less than 25% of their students care about classwork.
As many as 30% of college students say they are not
happy with the whole experience. They're there because they think they have to be to find jobs. Yet most
college graduates find jobs that have little or no
relationship to their major. Only professional training
in accounting or business administration or engineer-
ing, it would seem, prepares a person for future work.
Some believe that the only thing a traditional liberal
arts education provides is a diploma.

The diploma does make a difference in lifetime
earnings. But it's not necessarily that good an invest-

ment. Suppose you're interested in cars. You get a job after high school at a local garage, take courses while you work, and become a master mechanic. By the time your class graduates from college, you may be making more each year than the graduates will earn. But there's another consideration. Let's suppose you invest the money you saved for college. By age 65 that nest egg could have earned enough to more than equal the difference in earnings expected from the degree! It's even possible that you might take that money at age 30 or so, set up your own business, and really come out ahead.

Of course, what's important is that a person can enjoy his or her work and find it satisfying. That's much more important than a cash payoff. So probably the first question you need to ask yourself when you consider college is, do I really want to go? Or is it just that college is the thing everyone else does?

College certainly doesn't make a person intelligent or ambitious. It doesn't affect basic personality. And that diploma doesn't open as many vocational doors as it once did. For those who want job training, it's usually better to look at one of the many one- or two-year vocational training schools around. It simply may not be wise to invest time and money in a four-year holding pen, unless you really want to learn.

Choosing a college. These days anyone with average high school grades can make it into one of the more than 1,400 four-year schools in the United States. There's also the option of starting out at a convenient, inexpensive two-year community college, within commuting distance of home.

You can get information on colleges from several publications. *The College Handbook* is published by the College Entrance Examination Board and describes some 2,800 two- and four-year schools. Barron's Educational Services publishes *Profiles of American Colleges*. When looking through them for your school, look for costs, location, facilities, etc. It's a good idea to select perhaps a dozen possibilities and write for catalogs. Then look carefully at courses offered, descriptions of the program and campus, and compare the credentials of the faculty (listed in the back of most catalogs). This process should help you narrow your choices down to a half-dozen or less.

You'll find it's worthwhile to visit schools. This will help you and your parents get a feel for the campus atmosphere and give you an opportunity to talk together about college goals. Talk to students and visit a few classes. Are the students friendly? What is their evaluation of the school? Ask administrators how many students typically go on to graduate school or professional schools. A high percentage may indicate a competitive academic atmosphere. You'll discover that other schools have the reputation of being "party schools," where academics take a back seat to social life. All this information will help you choose a college that fits your own personal values and goals.

It may seem like a lot of bother to go through the kind of process described here. Some may decide just to attend Mom's or Dad's alma mater, or others may decide to cut costs, live at home, and attend a local community college. For the rest though, doing some research will be wise. After all, college will cost the family thousands of dollars. And cost you four years of your life!

What about a Christian college? Many parents want their children to attend a Christian college. And many young people want to go to a school where they'll be sure of Christian friends and where they will have a chance to think more seriously about their faith. Before you make a quick decision, here are facts to consider:

• Bible colleges. This is one type of Christian school. Bible colleges offer liberal arts courses but tend to stress study of the Bible, theology, and other Christian subject areas. Many offer majors designed for those who intend to go into some kind of full-time ministry, such as missions or youth work or teaching in the Christian day school. Many may find a Bible college the best place for them.

• Christian liberal arts colleges. These schools emphasize traditional liberal arts curriculums. They usually require a minimum number of courses in Bible, theology, and Christian ethics, as well as courses in the discipline the student chooses, whether it be philosophy, history, the physical sciences, languages, etc. Lifestyle on campus will vary with the school's religious heritage. It is important, therefore, to investigate the spiritual atmosphere of the campus when seeking a Christian school.

• Secular schools. It's a mistake to think of the secular campus as "godless." A number of organizations (like InterVaristy Christian Fellowship) have chapters on college and university campuses. Local churches in college towns may have active college groups. Some denominations will have campus ministers to provide counseling, fellowship, and Bible studies for students. Many young people have found that life on the secular campus forces them to seriously evaluate their own values and to deepen their personal commitment.

COMPETITION

America has a long-standing love affair with competition. We envision a West won by rugged families and individuals who dared to match themselves against vast distances and hostile natives. We see competition as the force that keeps the wheels of industry turning. Competitive sports fascinate us. And winning—whether by getting better grades or becoming Miss Arizona—is a primary way by which we measure achievement.

But these days there are growing doubts about competition. How do the Japanese, who stress cooperation, produce less expensive (and some say better) cars? Do competitive sports really build character? Or do they produce immature, irresponsible "jocks," whose egos demand a larger contract than the next player, no matter how ridiculous the salary? And we wonder. Can we really equate winning with achievement? Or is it a greater achievement for a person with limited abilities to pull down a "B" by hard work than for the class valedictorian to make an "A" without effort?

Questions like these make it worthwhile to take a look at competition and the role it plays in shaping our outlook on life.

Economic and political competition. A competitive marketplace for goods and ideas has a positive impact on society. Competition forces innovation and economy: prices are kept within reason, and new products emerge to meet needs and satisfy wants. In the same way political competition encourages citizens to weigh different ideas and to express their ideas with the vote. Economic and political competition can be misused. But the system of open competition is superior to other systems we might adopt.

Athletic competition. Athletics shifts our focus from competition for allegiance to goods or ideas to competition between persons. Here it's not the best washing machine or the conservative principle that wins, but human beings.

Most of us can and do enjoy friendly competition. But what happens to the personality of those who go on to higher, more intense levels of athletic competition? And what happens to all those who drop out because they were never good enough? The Institute for the Study of Athletic Motivation provides some answers to that first question. Their findings make it clear that competition does *not* build character. Actually there are common traits found in those who are winners. They have a great need for achievement; they are highly organized, dominant, and respectful of authority; and they have a capacity for trust. But they show low interest in receiving support and concern from others, nor do they indicate a need to take care of others. Competition seems to block the development of close affiliation with other people.

Competitiveness in general. Sports are an intense forum for competition, but society encourages the competitive approach to life in general. We compete for jobs and promotions. Usually our success comes at someone else's expense. Competition is stressed in schools, where grading and classroom activities constantly force students to measure themselves against others. One educator describes a situation in which Boris, a student, is unable to answer a math problem, even with the teacher's gentle prompting. So the teacher calls on Peggy, who is eagerly waving her hand for attention. Because Boris failed, Peggy is able to succeed. His disappointment is the occasion for her rejoicing. The principle of measuring ourselves against the successes or failures of others is deeply ingrained in society. People compete with each other beginning in childhood. And for every winner, there will be losers as well.

The biblical perspective. The ancient Greek poet Homer brought the nature of competition into focus when he urged "always to strive for distinction and surpass the others." This is the value in the competitive approach: surpassing others. Its roots are not just to be found in American society but in the heart of natural man. But this whole approach to life is challenged in Scripture, and a different system of values put in its place. We see the Bible's system in several New Testament passages.

• Romans 12:3 says, "Do not think of yourself more highly than you ought." Each believer "belongs to all the others" and is to use his or her different gifts and abilities to serve.

• First Corinthians 4:6 warns against taking "pride in one man over against another." Again the point is, that God intentionally makes each of us different for the purposes of service. Differences are not to be twisted into hierarchies of superiority/inferiority.

• Second Corinthians 10:12–13 ridicules the foolishness of leaders who classify and compare themselves with others in an empty attempt to establish authority.

• Philippians 2:3, 4 calls for an attitude marked by unity of spirit and purpose. "Do nothing out of selfish ambition or vain conceit, but in humility consider others better than yourselves. Each of you should look not only at your own interests, but also to the interests of others."

• Galatians 6:4 calls on each person to test his own actions, "then he can take pride in himself, without comparing himself to somebody else."

These passages make it clear. We are to strive to serve others, not surpass them. We are to appreciate the strengths of others, not build ourselves up by measuring our strengths against their weaknesses. And finally, we are to excel so that we can take pride in our faithfulness, and not to lift ourselves above our brothers and sisters.

Excelling without competitive drive. Christianity puts great stress on faithfulness and on excelling in our zeal to follow Christ. How do we strive for excellence without competitiveness?

• Establish impersonal, reachable goals. When my oldest child was in grade school we played Jarts (large metal darts, thrown across the backyard to land in plastic circles). Paul's frustration grew as he tried harder and harder to beat me . . . and failed. He competed furiously and the losing hurt. So I made a simple change in the game. We combined our scores and then set ourselves the task each round of trying to beat our record high. This simple shift changed the dynamics of the game. We still competed, but we tried to surpass ourselves and our past achievements, not each other.

• Praise and appreciate differences. Do not compare friends or family members with yourself. Focus on the strengths, interests, and achievements of others. When we help people appreciate their own uniqueness we help them see ways they can contribute to others. This does not require denying our own strengths and achievements. In fact, we don't have to rule out all friendly competition as though winning and losing were themselves sin. They're not. What is wrong is the kind of competitive attitude that shapes our view of ourselves and others by demanding that to be worthwhile we must surpass others.

Actually the ones who struggle to surpass and fail are not so much the losers as those who are the apparent winners in life—the athletic, the attractive, the rich, the popular. They are often the most insecure. A person who defines himself or herself in terms of the ability to surpass others is under a lot of stress. And he or she is not free.

And so we stand again amazed at the wisdom of God. In freeing us from the need to measure ourselves against others, He has freed us to love and to be loved. And in this freedom, God has met our deepest needs.

CONFLICT AND RESOLUTION

It's a pretty safe prediction: there will be some conflict in your life today.

What are the principal causes of conflict? Misunderstanding (as when communication fails). Personality clashes. Value and goal differences. Poor performance. Conflicts over who is responsible for what. Authority issues. Frustration and irritability. Competition for limited resources. Failure to keep rules and policies.

Conflicts like these are a normal part of everyone's life. There is no way to avoid them. So the issue becomes how we deal with conflicts. Do we approach conflict constructively, so growth takes place in our lives and relationships? Or is our approach to conflict destructive, tearing down relationships and blocking our personal growth?

Resolving conflicts. Those who have studied conflict resolution point to four things that are important to evaluate.

• Evaluate your own reaction to conflict. Here are the most common reactions people have when some conflict emerges. Out of all these responses only two of them are really positive. (1) We react by trying to justify ourselves. "Yes, but . . ." (2) We react by expressing hostility and fighting back. (3) We react by changing the subject and trying to divert attention from the issue in question. "Let's talk about it later. Right now let's . . ." (4) We react by trying to avoid the issue entirely. "Well, that's no problem for me." (5) We react by trying to smooth the conflict over. "I think we're both right, and . . ." (6) We react by surrender. "You're perfectly right. It's all my fault. Can you ever forgive me?" (7) We react by expressing our feelings. "When you say that, I feel . . ." (8) We react by attempting to negotiate. "Let's work on it and see if we can find a solution."

If we're to deal with conflict constructively, we can't avoid or deny conflicts. And we can't defend ourselves, attack, or even surrender. We need to be willing to talk, to share our feelings, and to work toward some solution that will meet everyone's needs.

• Evaluate your communication. To deal with conflict constructively and to find real solutions each person must express his or her true thoughts and feelings. And it's vital that each person listens.

• Evaluate the relational climate. The relational climate is the overall quality of relationships. Do those in conflict see and treat each other with mutual affection and respect? Where warmth and caring exist, there's a good chance of finding solutions. Where suspicion and lack of trust dominate, conflicts are likely to become destructive.

• Evaluate the methods used to resolve conflicts. Experts focus attention on five common methods. (1) Denial. One or both parties try to solve the conflict by pretending it does not exist. This works with insignificant conflicts and in fact reflects the Bible's observation that when we love we "forebear" (overlook) one another's sins (cf. Col. 3:13). However, when the issue is important to one or both parties, denying that the conflict exists leads to a buildup of tensions and can be destructive to the relationship. (2) Smoothing over. One or both work at maintaining a superficial, surface harmony. But underneath, suppressed resentment will build. Like denial, this is a refusal to deal honestly with the conflict and will ultimately be destructive. (3) Power. Here one person or group dominates and simply imposes his or her solution. The power approach may work in the military where everyone agrees to obey orders. But in relationships, a person is made to feel powerless. Parents may be tempted to use this approach on their children, but again, it can be destructive. (4) Compromise. Each person surrenders something so each can gain. This attempt to find a middle ground will work when each feels he or she has room to give a little and where there is mutual trust. (5) Collaboration. All parties work together to seek a creative solution to meet the needs of all. Collaboration calls for time, for honest communication, and for concern for the point of view of all parties, and is the best way to work on solutions to conflict over really important matters.

Biblical insights. While secular experts focus attention on our reaction to conflict, the Bible calls us to take a closer look at ourselves. The Book of James points to the inner cause of many conflicts. "If you harbor bitter envy and selfish ambition in your hearts," James writes, "do not boast about it or deny the truth. Such 'wisdom' does not come down from heaven but is earthly, unspiritual, of the devil. For where you have envy and selfish ambition, there you find disorder and every evil practice. But the wisdom that comes from heaven is first of all pure; then peace-loving, considerate, submissive, full of mercy and good fruit, impartial and sincere" (3:14–17). When the roots of conflict are located in our own sinful desires, the place to deal with it is in our own lives. We can confess uncovered sins and trust God to cleanse, filling us with a wisdom that leads to peace.

Then is conflict itself wrong? No. At times conflict is necessary. Galatians describes a conflict between Paul and Peter. Peter had come to visit an all-Gentile church. When some legalistic believers came later, Peter drew back and separated himself from the Gentile Christians, as Jews had always separated themselves from pagans. Paul saw this as denial of the gospel, which offers salvation to all by faith alone. Because the issue was so vital, Paul confronted Peter "in front of them all." Later the issue was dealt with by the whole church in a council at Jerusalem (Acts 15). This conflict was a vital and positive element in the struggle of the early church to grasp the meaning of the new Christian faith.

But even the apostle Paul was not immune to destructive conflicts. He fell out with his old missionary companion, Barnabas, when Barnabas wanted to bring along John Mark, a young man who deserted the missionary team on an earlier journey. Paul gave priority to the mission: Barnabas gave priority to strengthening John Mark. The Bible tells us that they were in such sharp disagreement that they parted company (see Acts 15:36–41). But Paul had been wrong. Barnabas did take Mark along, and under the guidance of this older brother Mark became an effective leader . . . and author of the gospel bearing his name (cf. 2 Tim. 4:11).

What we learn from passages like these is important. We are taught to examine our own attitude first; not to avoid conflict when issues are important to us; to guard humility; and finally, when we seem to fail, to know that God brings good through conflict.

CONVERSION

I could feel the anguish in the two letters I received this year from a Tennessee teen. He had asked Jesus to save him. But he didn't feel saved. How could he ever be sure?

The Bible on conversion. Both Testaments picture conversion as a fundamental change in life direction. Moved by God (Jer. 18:8; John 6:44), a person turns his or her back on evil and chooses a new way of life (Jer. 18:11; Mal. 3:7). The convert rejects the old dominion of sin and chooses Jesus as Lord (Rom. 6:11–14). Growing in personal commitment to Christ, the new believer develops a new outlook and new values; he or she begins to understand and choose God's will (cf. Rom. 12:1, 2). This new life, supernaturally planted in the believer by God, is the dynamic source of all changes in attitude and action (cf. Jer. 31:33). The word most closely linked with conversion is faith. There is God's act of implanting life; there is faith in Christ; and there is growth and change as we accept the lordship of Christ and begin a life of obedience to Him.

Our conversion experience. Christians often seem confused about the conversion "experience." It's no wonder. Some insist we name the date and hour we received Jesus as Savior. Others argue that children should be nurtured in faith from infancy, so they're never aware of a time they were unconverted. Some will tell us of several moments of significant personal decision. And others, like my young Tennessee friend, will wonder why, no matter how many times he makes his "decision for Christ," he still doesn't feel converted. How do we sort it all out?

• We affirm a point of conversion, a moment when God provides us supernaturally with a new life (cf. 1 Peter 1:23).

• We affirm faith as a personal response to God, as the human responsibility in conversion (cf. John 3:16).

• We admit not all Christians are aware of the moment of conversion. I can't remember the moment of my physical birth, but I know I'm alive. The real issue for individuals is not "When was I saved?" but "Do I believe in Jesus?" Answer that second question "Yes," and you know you're alive.

• We separate feelings and fact. I am not converted because I feel converted. The Bible says, "To all who received him [Jesus], to those who believed in his name, he gave the right to become children of God" (John 1:12). The fact is, faith in Jesus brings us into God's family, and we have God's word on that. My confidence rests on the promise of a God whose word I trust, not on feelings that I know to be fickle.

• We understand that transformation is generally gradual and involves growth. Conversion will lead to *eventual* rejection of evil and choosing of what is good. "No one who is born of God will continue to sin," the Bible promises, "because God's seed remains in him; he cannot go on sinning, because he has been born of God" (1 John 3:9).

Talk of conversion should not direct our attention into the past, to establish the point of time when our life in Christ began. The good news of conversion is that in Jesus the old is gone. We can look ahead with confidence, all has become new.

COUNSELING

New counseling centers open. Christian bookstores stock counseling books and cassette series. Pastors are overloaded with counseling. Marriage and family counselors advertise in the yellow pages. Churches hold training courses to equip lay counselors. And many of us wonder. What's this movement all about? Here's some information to help you sort through the complex idea of counseling in general.

Types of counseling. Two decades ago the word "psychological" would normally have been linked with counseling. Counseling was for people with personal problems, who wanted help. But today the term "counseling" includes much more.

• Psychological counseling. People still seek counseling for help with personal and personality problems.

At times life seems so overwhelming that insights and help from outside are simply necessary.

• Behavioral counseling. "Stop Smoking" and "Diet" centers so popular these days are actually counseling centers. They use techniques developed by behaviorists to help an individual change patterns in his or her life. What a person does, not how he or she feels, is the focus in behavioral counseling.

• Employment and educational counseling. Batteries of tests are used to help individuals determine the kind of schooling or work they are suited for and will enjoy.

• Marriage and family counseling. Closely knit groups of people are counseled together as a unit. The counseling focuses on the way the persons interact. The counselor helps the group members become more sensitive to each other and introduces concepts that can change destructive patterns.

• Group counseling. Groups of persons with similar problems (such as child-abusing parents or alcoholics) are brought together regularly. The group members talk through experiences, to learn ways to change, and to provide each other with encouragement and support.

Theories of counseling. The counseling process in any of the settings above will depend on the counseling theory applied by the counselor. There are five major theory groups that are more or less in vogue:

• Reflective. The counselor sees himself or herself as an outsider. The counselor is there only to act as a mirror, reflecting and clarifying the thoughts, feelings, and values of the counselee. The counselor believes that each individual must ultimately solve his or her own problems, and resists trying to instruct or direct the counselee.

• Relational. The counselor views the counselor-counselee relationship that develops as therapeutic. Caring and being supportive are vital in his or her approach to counseling.

• Insight. The counselor believes the counselee needs insights he or she does not possess. So the counselor will draw from studies and expertise, and provide information during the counseling process that will better help the counselee understand himself or herself and the situation.

• Directive. The counselor believes the counselee needs answers and that the counselor's role is to provide them. After listening carefully to define the problem, the directive counselor will then tell the counselee what to do.

• Behavioral. The counselor is not concerned with what goes on inside the counselee. The focus is on specific patterns of behavior that cause the problem. By teaching the counselee how to act to change personal behavior patterns, the counselor believes he or she can help the counselee solve the problems.

Today there are few "pure" practitioners of any of these theory groups, and a counselor will likely draw techniques from each school. Still most counselors will tend to rely on one approach as his or her dominant method.

Biblical perspectives on counseling. The New Testament does not speak of counseling as we understand it today, nor does it list counseling among the spiritual gifts. But there is much in the Scriptures that is clearly related.

• "One anothering." The Bible words translated "counselor" in the New International Version are used most often in the sense of adviser. However, the use of Counselor by Jesus as a name for the Holy Spirit (John 14 and 15) is significant. The name sums up several of the Spirit's ministries and means "one who comes alongside as a helper." The Bible also describes how believers in the Christian community were constantly "alongside" and "helping" one another. Believers shared sorrows and joys. They encouraged, reproved, rebuked, exhorted, taught, listened to, forgave, prayed for, and stimulated one another to growth. There was no need for professional or specialized counselors.

• Christ as Lord. Helping is presented in Scripture as a mutual ministry in which brothers and sisters in Christ offer each other support. One possible danger in counseling as we understand it today is that it often involves a superior/subordinate relationship in which the counselor is perceived to be superior or "over" the counselee. This is particularly true in directive counseling, where the counselor takes it as his or her responsibility to tell the counselee what to do.

The New Testament makes it clear that Jesus alone is Lord, and each of us is to seek direction from Him. We are to relate to each other as brothers and sisters only, resisting titles and status that might seem to raise us above others (cf. Matt. 23:8–12). We can make suggestions, share our insights, and provide encouragement. But each individual is to remain personally responsible to Christ for what he or she chooses to do.

• Developing sensitivity. The present movement that encourages Christians to take training in counseling—a training that usually stresses how to listen and encourage—is a healthy thing. In every field, evidence mounts that peer counseling (by nonprofessionals) can be as or more effective than professional counseling. Building a congregation of people who understand how to care may well help us recover the healing, transforming power that once prevailed in the church.

Conclusions. Everyone needs help at times. That help often will come from friends or family, or a small group of other Christians with whom we meet for prayer and Bible study. Professional counselors can help too, and it's no shame to seek help. When you do seek pastoral or professional counseling, try to get some idea of the counselor's approach. Generally speaking, the reflective and directive approaches will be the least helpful. The behavioral can help when you are trying to lick a crippling habit. It is also helpful if people you can trust recommend someone who has a good record of success. But don't overlook the possibility that people in your congregation are sensitive and caring, and that talking things through with a brother or sister may be just the help you need.

DECISION MAKING

Many of the decisions you and I make are irrelevant. Wear blue today or brown? Eggs or cereal for breakfast? For decisions like these, we can just ask ourselves, "Do I want to . . . ?" If the answer is yes, do it. If no, don't. But there are other decisions where the instant approach—the "I want" approach—will not work.

• Direction-setting decisions. These are important choices because we know they will set the direction of our future. "Shall I marry Beth?" and "Shall I quit my job?" are direction setters. Decisions that affect our future requires more than an "I want" approach; they require judgment. A good question to ask is, "Will this direction be right and satisfying for me? Shall I do it then?" Hesitancy tells you you're undecided and that you need to gather more information and let your decision ride.

• Moral decisions. Some decisions are a matter of morality. Again the "want to" approach is inadequate. Now the question becomes "Is X right or wrong?" It's not always easy to sort out moral issues. Our thinking can be confused by the (not necessarily correct) opinions of others and by the (not necessarily correct) content of our own conscience. When we are uncertain, it's important to search Scripture for moral guidelines and to ask God to guide us through the gray areas. If we determine that the thing we question is all right morally, then we're back to the "Do I want to . . ." question.

• Patterning decisions. Sometimes "want to" kinds of things, with no moral component and no life-shaping impact, fall into patterns. "Do I want to watch TV?" is an appropriate, morally neutral "want to" kind of thing. But if we answer yes *every* evening and watching TV becomes a time-consuming habit that affects our lifestyle, a new issue has been raised.

It's helpful every now and then to look at the pattern of our irrelevant decisions. "Do I want that snack?" "Do I want to skip exercise today?" "Do I want to sleep an extra half-hour?" Each decision alone may seem unimportant, but as one in a series of decisions, it may deserve our closer attention.

Putting it all together, these three questions may provide a simple key to personal decision making.

"Do I want to?" is sufficient for most daily chores.

"Shall I?" is for those serious, direction-setting decisions.

"Should I?" comes into play whenever we think there is a moral issue involved. And every now and then we need to look at the pattern of our "want to" choices, to see if we need to shift some into the "shall I?" or the "should I?" categories.

What about finding God's will. Christians are rightly concerned about finding God's will when they are making decisions. How does God fit into the pattern I've suggested? Beautifully and (super)naturally.

Assuming that you are a believer who is willing to do God's will, you can be confident that God Himself is committed to guiding you through life. Paul puts it this way in Philippians: "It is God who works in you to will and to act according to his good purpose" (2:13). Christ has taken up residence in your life: He is at work in your decision-making process.

Several things strengthen the role of God in your decision making and help you make that process more effective.

• Your time in Scripture. God has filled His Word with precepts and principles (general guidelines) that help us understand His outlook on the issues of life. The better you understand the Word and the deeper your insights into God's values, the better your decisions will become.

• Your sharing with others. God intends us to live in fellowship with other brothers and sisters. That's the whole point of His great invention, the church. We're not to ask others to make our decisions for us. But as we share together, we can learn much from others' experiences and counsel. The closer your relationship with God's people, the better your decisions will become.

• Your conscious reliance on God. God does not direct us in an audible voice or with a shouted imperative. But as long as you and I maintain an attitude of awareness of God's involvement and of our dependence on Him, we can be sure the Lord will guide us. "Commit your way to the LORD," the psalmist promises, "trust in him and he will do this: he will make your righteousness shine like the dawn, the justice of your cause like the noonday sun" (Ps. 37:–5, 6).

When you are growing in your grasp of Scripture

and in your fellowship with God's people, and when you commit your way to the Lord, He will guide your answers to the "want to," "shall I," and "should I" questions of your life.

DISCIPLESHIP

So you want to be a disciple but don't know just how to go about it? Some today suggest you link up with a more mature Christian who will "disciple" you. This person will meet with you each week, give you assignments, and review your Bible study and daily decisions. Other people suggest you take a course. Or read a particular book. One leader I know tells you to listen to his cassettes. Pow! Instant disciples.

Not a program, a relationship. Jesus' Great Commission tells us to "make disciples of all nations" (Matt. 28:19). This is a call to a relationship with Jesus, not to establish another church program. We realize that discipleship is for all believers, requiring active obedience: "Everything I have commanded" is to flow (28:20). Both Old and New Testaments link obedience with love: "If anyone loves me, he will obey my teaching" (John 14:23, 24; Deut. 11:18, 22). A disciple then is a believer in a growing personal relationship with the Lord, which results in deepening love and obedience.

Disciple-making. Two New Testament pictures help us understand how to make disciples. Each description is geared to the personal transformation of the individual (cf. Luke 6:40). In the Gospels we see Jesus making disciples. He chooses a group of a dozen and works closely with them for some three years. They stay close to Him, hear His teaching, discuss, ask and are asked questions, and are sent out together to minister to others. Living together and sharing experiences under Jesus' guidance, they become disciples.

In the Epistles we see the church making disciples. Again believers are called together in intimate groups. These groups stay close together and build close, loving relationships. Their members teach and admonish each other (Col. 3:16). As more mature believers are recognized as spiritual leaders, they provide teaching and living examples for our life of faith (cf. 1 Peter 5:3; 1 Tim. 4:12; Phil. 4:9). Living together and sharing experiences, believers become disciples.

Discipleship today. Today as in Bible times, discipleship is for all believers. And disciples are made by the same process. The secret is not a one-on-one relationship or a special course. The secret is simply living together as the church, the people of God, in intimate relationship. Together we share study, life, and prayer. And together we become disciples.

ELOPING

It sounds so romantic. And for some, it can be. But there are several questions worth asking before climbing down that moonlit ladder. For instance: (1) Is the person you plan to elope with an attractive stranger, or is this the culmination of a long-term, growing relationship? (2) Is the idea a spur-of-the-moment thing, or have you talked through the pros and cons? (3) Are you both more or less alone? Or are there relatives and friends who'd be disappointed not to share the wedding with you? (4) What are your reasons for preferring eloping to a traditional wedding?

Eloping can be a special and exciting way to begin a marriage, so I hope all these questions haven't spoiled the romantic mood for you. But if it's only a romantic mood, and you haven't thought through questions like these, maybe it wasn't such a good idea anyway.

EMOTIONS

Emotions seem both a plague and a joy. We're troubled by our emotions and enriched by them. Sometimes our emotions seem uncontrollable: they force us into actions we later regret. Other times emotions drop us toward despair, leading us to doubt our relationship with God. But what can a person do? Emotions exist. We can't deny them. Enriching and troubling, emotions are something we each need to understand and get in healthy perspective.

Why emotions? God is the One who made us able to feel. He placed in us a full range of emotions, from exhilaration and quiet satisfaction to guilt and burning anger. Emotions were necessary if God was to accomplish the goal of making creatures in His image (Gen. 1:26, 27). God also is a person. The Bible speaks often of His love, His compassion, His enjoyment of the good and His anger at evil. So our emotions reflect something of the Person who shaped us to be like Him. Our feelings give us some insight into what God is like. It's hard to imagine God as some impersonal force or indifferent cosmic mathematician. God is a person who can and who does love.

But while our emotional make-up reflects our Creator, that reflection is distorted by sin. We often link our feelings to wrong objects. We can actually enjoy sin and feel contempt for what is beautiful and good. God is the source of our ability to feel. But He is not responsible for the specific emotions we experience. This means that emotions are not always a trustworthy guide to living. "I want it" doesn't make something right. And "I like it" doesn't make it good.

Limitations on emotions. The fact that emotions are not a trustworthy guide is only one of their limitations. Even though emotions may feel so strong and real, they are poor indicators of reality.

Imagine a husband who is feeling hurt and upset at being neglected by his wife. "The baby gets all her attention," he mutters to himself. As for his wife, she's depressed and exhausted. And the silent treatment she's been getting from her suddenly uncommunicative husband makes her feel rejected. She's worried too that since the baby has arrived he doesn't find her attractive anymore. All these feelings are authentic.

But suppose they talk. Suppose he shares how

he's been feeling, and with relief she tells him of her fears. For the first time he realizes how exhausted she must be. He gives her a warm hug and insists she go take a nap while he takes care of their baby. Suddenly new, warm, and loving feelings rush in and replace the old feelings. These new feelings also are authentic.

There are several things we see about the limitations of our emotions in this illustration. Emotions are not a trustworthy guide to what is right or to what is good for us. But also:

• Emotions may not be appropriate to the realities of any given situation.

• Emotions can—and will—change. They are not stable or reliable guides.

Knowing these things about emotions, we can see why it's important not to let our emotions rule us or to rely on our emotions in evaluating situations. Oh, our emotions are real to us all right. And often powerful. But to live by the push and pull of momentary, changeable, and unreliable feelings is a very dangerous way to live.

Living with our emotions. We may not want to live by our emotions. But we do have to live with them. So how can we do that in a healthy and positive way? Several principles help us.

• Accept ownership of your emotions. Don't blame others or the situation. No one "makes" you feel as you do.

For instance, a teenager had an auto accident soon after getting his license—right after Dad's lecture on safe driving, and when Dad heard about it, he was understandably mad. It would be wrong to say the accident "made" him mad. He could have reacted differently. For instance, he might have given his son a hug and told him how thankful he felt that the boy wasn't hurt.

• Express emotions to God. The psalms teach us this. God invites us to share our positive and negative feelings with Him. Freely. He already knows how we feel and still accepts and loves us. We can't shock Him. When we share our emotions with Him, He will enrich the emotions that are enjoyable and gradually transform the emotions that might lead us into sin.

Read through the psalms and you'll see how this works. Jot down feeling words: see how every emotion you've known is shared with the Lord. And note how God gently works within the psalmists to turn thoughts to Him, gradually modifying emotions to bring peace.

• Avoid ventilation of emotions. Recent theory suggests a person gets rid of emotions by expressing them. Even angry verbal attacks on others are justified by taking them as a sign of "honesty."

Actually, research has shown that ventilation doesn't work. Shouting and kicking chairs when you're angry won't make you a less angry person: it will probably just make you able to express anger in destructive ways. Dumping your feelings on a person isn't honesty, it's simply expressing hostility. While it is good to talk about your anger, just be sure it is your feelings you're discussing and not the other person's shortcomings.

• Stand in judgment over your emotions. Emotions are real, and we have to deal with them. But we don't have to be dominated by them. To avoid this, begin with the realization that your feelings are not, in themselves, sin. Anger isn't sin in itself, rather it's the acts that anger prompts that can be sinful.

As a matter of fact, anger can be an occasion for significant moral victory. A friend of mine was viciously attacked by a woman in his Bible-study group. She attacked his motives and behavior, and hurled charges at other group members as well, then marched out of the house. My friend was hurt and angry. But the next morning he followed Jesus' instructions and sought a reconciliation. He apologized to her for any hurts and shared his feelings without casting blame.

What happened here? The negative emotion of anger surged in my friend. But he stood in judgment over his emotion, refusing to react negatively. Instead he was obedient to Jesus and took the first step toward reconciliation, despite his own hurt. The "wrong" emotion, rather than leading my friend to sin, actually led him to make a series of godly choices that strengthened him in his Christian commitment, and which brought glory to God.

Conclusions. Long ago Martin Luther suggested you can't keep birds from flying around your head, but you can surely keep them from building a nest in your hair. Emotions are like this. They can cause a fury in our lives at times, but we can choose which emotion we will act on and which we will not.

And we can express every feeling to God, knowing He understands and cares. As we submit daily to His will, our emotional life will come increasingly under His loving control.

ENGAGEMENT

While there are no specific biblical instructions for us concerning engagement, it is an important step leading to marriage. Because so many marriages end in divorce today, it should be a time for developing a deeper understanding of each other. The engagement calls for exploring temperament and personal qualities carefully. It's helpful for an engaged couple to participate in a marriage preparation course or to have premarital counseling. Engagement isn't a time for playing at being married. In fact, a couple must be open to the possibility that this examination could lead them to call the wedding off.

How long should the engagement be? There's no definitive answer. But one word of advice Paul gives in Thessalonians is helpful. He writes about acquiring a wife "in holiness and honor, not in the passion of lust like heathen who do not know God" (4:5 RSV). Paul is not against sex. But he knows passion is only part of marriage and should never force us into hasty action. Couples do need to take time to come to know each other well to establish a strong foundation for a lasting marriage. The time required? However long it takes you to come to know each other well and to be certain about each other.

EXPECTATIONS

Christianity has a tremendous impact on our expectations. We know the past does not lock anyone into a predetermined tomorrow and that in Christ we have reason to expect the good, not the bad: the best, not the worst, from ourselves and from others. A pastor once put it this way. "People need us to believe for them, until they're able to believe for themselves." You see, Christian faith isn't just something long ago or far away. Christian faith is fixed in a living God, who is committed to us in Christ, and who *knows* (not just expects) that we will become the very best we can be, in Him (cf. 2 Cor. 5:21).

FAILURE

Like death and taxes, we can expect failure. And failure is about as welcome. But failure isn't a problem in itself: it's how we deal with it. Abe Lincoln was a political failure. He never won an office for which he ran . . . until he won the presidency.

Some of us have been anxious about failing. We worked hard to get out of doing school work because we were so afraid of failing. So we simply did not try. Life holds many terrors for those afraid to fail. Some of us had no one to help us with failure when we were children. And we may be troubled and afraid to try now. What can we do? We can let God parent us and rebuild our confidence. After all, God deals with our sins (those *real* failures of ours) calmly and lovingly (cf. Ps. 103:8–14). Look at the experiences of Peter reported in the Gospels. He tried hard and with enthusiasm. Yet he often failed, and Jesus had to correct or restrain him. Yet Jesus never rejected the bumbling disciple. In the end he became one of the most productive Christian leaders.

Let God guide you in little daily steps of obedience. Don't dream of big victories. Just seek to be faithful in one little thing a day. Remember that God doesn't berate you when you fail.

FAME

Ever thought much about what makes people famous? People can be famous because of their looks (Brooke Shields), their name (Rockefeller), a discovery they've made (Salk), because they're familiar to us (Walter Cronkite), or because they're entertaining (Bill Cosby). They may be famous because they're athletic (Pete Rose) or have held a high position (Kissinger). But think about fame—it's fleeting. A hundred years from now some will not even have heard of the names I've listed. Doubt it? Try listing 1880s personalities that were famous for looks, name, discovery, familiarity, entertainment, sports, or position.

FEAR

Is it all right to be afraid? Or should a Christian "trust"? And what about the "fear of the Lord"? How does it fit in?

Some of our fears are related to real threats. Fire burns, and we must learn not to touch it. Adults presented with frightening information on smoking tend to cut down. A person going into the hospital with some fear tends to bear up better under the actual experience than a person who has denied or repressed such fears. These fears are helpful, even spiritually beneficial, for they give the believer fresh opportunities to trust God (Ps. 56:3) and be delivered from panic (56:4). After all, "trust" is meaningless if there is nothing to fear.

Several practices can help us deal with fears related to real threats to ourselves and to our loved ones. These are:

• Accept the fact of the threat, and do not try to deny it.

• Accept your own feelings of fear as legitimate.

• Gather information that will help you deal with the threat realistically. For instance if you're going into the hospital, find out as much as you can from the doctor about medical procedures, how much pain you can expect to have, etc. Knowing what to expect can help avoid panic.

• Express your fears and trust in God. Let Him deal with your panic, just as He provided reassurance to the psalmists. God is not angry with us for feeling fear:

He knows that fears give us opportunity to learn that we can trust Him.

There's another kind of fear, strange as it may seem, that God offers: a freeing fear. We read in the Bible, "The fear of the LORD is the beginning of wisdom" (Prov. 9:10). If we stand in awe of God, the fears that have us bound and which can often lead us to do evil will be seen in perspective.

Jesus taught the crowds who came to hear Him, "Do not be afraid of those who kill the body and after that can do no more. But I will show you whom you should fear: Fear him who, after the killing of the body, has power to throw you into hell. Yes, I tell you, fear him" (Luke 12:4, 5). Awareness of God and His awesome power is intended to release us from bondage to our terror of others.

FELLOWSHIP

In the modern church fellowship is likely to mean "social get together." But in the early church it meant "participation": a sharing of life, rooted in the believer's relationship with Jesus and, because of Jesus, with other Christians (cf. 1 Cor. 1:9; Phil. 1:5).

"Fellowship" in the Bible is a bold, vibrant word that is powerfully affirming. It tells us we each have a share in Jesus' continuing work on earth as well as in the benefits of His death and resurrection. Fellowship focuses on the fact that we believers have a share in one another's lives. The word "fellowship" ("share") is even chosen to describe the Christian's weekly contribution of money and talents.

It is most impressive to read through the New Testament and sense how intimate is the shared life in Christ; there is the giving and receiving of counsel, encouragement, forgiveness, concern, instruction, correction, and, most of all, love. We discover an openness that comes when believers realize they're truly accepted. There is in Christ a fellowship that breaks through the barrier of loneliness that isolates people, and delight comes from being together and sharing joys, as well as sorrows.

FREEDOM

Most of us make the mistake of connecting the word "freedom" with "from." We say "free speech" and mean freedom from censorship. We say "free press" and mean freedom from government control. Even when adolescents cry out "I want to be free!" what they usually mean is free from restrictions imposed by school or parents. They want to do what *they* want to do, when they want to do it.

All this talk of freedom is deceptive, because we humans are never really free "from" anything. Each of us lives in bondage to all sorts of limitations. Our bodies demand sleep; our work demands our time. We might insist on "freedom" and try to stay awake, or we might quit work and go fishing. But soon we would collapse from exhaustion or would run out of money.

Every choice we make carries consequences. We can make our choices and pretend to be free. But we can never be free from the consequences of our choices. The Christian concept of freedom is radical. In Christ we are not promised "freedom from," instead we are promised that through divinely designed restrictions we are freed to find what we yearn for: fulfillment and meaning in life. Slaves to Christ, we become truly free (cf. Rom. 6:15–23).

FRIENDSHIP

Friendships grow when we begin to trust another person, when we make ourselves vulnerable to another and reveal things about ourselves. If the person with whom we share ourselves responds with acceptance and with reciprocal self-disclosure, the relationship will deepen. If we share our thoughts and feelings and the other does not, we'll grow uncomfortable, and the friendship will remain superficial. Here are biblical guidelines for building friendships:

Friendship calls for acceptance. "Accept one another, then, just as Christ accepted you" (Rom. 15:7). There is no greater acceptance than this.

Friendship implies equality. We are all children of God and servants of one another. How can we be more equal?

Friendship calls for trust and self-revelation. Then to whom are we freer to bare our burdens than to those who care enough to bear them with us (Gal. 6:2)?

FULFILLMENT

Remember the Army recruitment ad, "Be all that you can be?" It seems that people are wrapped up in an intense search for self-fulfillment. And they search for it in their jobs, in accumulating material things, or even in the pursuit of "reaching their fullest potentiality" or "meeting their inner needs."

Where is true fulfillment to be found? Actually, the Christian's answer goes back to that army commercial. Fulfillment does come when we grow to "be all that we can be" in the context of our new life of faith.

"You have been given fullness in Christ," we are told in Colossians 2:10. We are also informed that God has given us a new life in Him. That new life isn't found in vain pursuits or by avoiding life's cares. It is lived by facing life, all the trivial things as well as the hassles, in a godly trusting way. The way James puts it, "whenever you face trials of many kinds . . . know that the testing of your faith develops perseverance. Perseverance must finish its work so that you may be mature and complete" (1:2, 3).

Being complete. That's fulfillment. That is being all that we can be.

GOAL SETTING

Everyone agrees we need to set goals. "Shoot at nothin' " an old farmer once said, "an' you'll be sure to hit it." When you do set goals, set them as guidelines, not masters. God may surprise us and change our schedule when we least expect it. Goals we set are to be maintained humbly. Jesus, not our goals, is Lord. (For a classic case, see Acts 8:4–8 and 8:26–29).

• Set goals for now, not years from now. Goals are helpful in developing discipline for present tasks. They help us live a day-by-day life of obedience.

• Set goals for yourself, not others. We can help others set goals but not by saying, "Here are the goals I have set for you." Goal-setting is a special but personal affair.

GRIEF

The kind of grief most common to us is when someone we loves dies. There are certain kinds of responses in the grieving process. There may be shock (a numbness or blank despair), disbelief, anger, and guilt feelings. There's likely to be crying.

During the mourning period a person may lose interest in work and other normal activities. The mourner may experience a sense of continued presence of the lost one. She or he may become ill. This acute grief generally spans about two weeks, although chronic grief may last for months or years.

The Bible views grief as a normal experience. But Scripture also adds that we do not "grieve like the rest of men, who have no hope" (1 Thess. 4:13). Sure that Jesus died and rose again, we know our loss is not permanent. We will meet our loved ones in the Lord when Christ returns.

Helping people who are grieving. Our society seeks to isolate us from death and too often we feel uncomfortable with another's pain. We withdraw rather than reach out to help others, because we don't quite know how to help. Here are several simple principles for helping others.

• Be there. Do not intrude, but let the grieving person know you are there and that you care.

• Remain open to the loss. Don't pretend nothing has happened or that the loss is not real. Express your own sorrow if you knew the other person well.

• Be sympathetic. Be willing to feel with and to talk with the grieving person about his or her feelings. Expression of feelings is a vital part of working through a loss.

• Encourage reminiscing. Talking about the past relationship with the person who has died helps to acknowledge the death, while affirming the vital part the deceased had in the griever's life.

• Affirm Christian hope. Believers will take comfort in a loved one's presence with the Lord and in a future reunion. There will still be grief. But the comforting truths of the gospel help bridge the initial period of intense sorrow.

Grief also brings a need to be alone, as well as need for support from warm and loving brothers and sisters. How good it is that in the family of God we can be sensitive to one another and minister lovingly. And how good that our grief always includes the affirmation of hope.

GUILT AND GUILT FEELINGS

Guilt is the result of our choosing, as responsible human beings, to do wrong. Guilt feelings are a gracious witness provided by God to the fact of our sin. Only when harmony between God and man is restored can an individual be really free from guilt. God's solution to guilt and guilt feelings is found in forgiveness, for it is by forgiveness He deals with sin. When God forgives sin He removes the root of guilt and lays a basis for the cleansing of our conscience. Hebrews 8 and 10 deal extensively with this great and wonderful revelation.

• Jesus' self-sacrificial death was payment for the penalty of sin. With sin paid for, neither sin nor guilt remain. "We have been made holy through the sacrifice of the body of Jesus Christ once for all" (10:10).

• It may take some time for us to experience the freeing power of forgiveness. Few transformations are immediate. But Christ's work does "cleanse our consciences from acts that lead to death, so that we may serve the living God" (9:14). As we are released from the heavy weight of our past, we grow into a renewed experience of life. Those feelings of guilt may persist after conversion, but there are several steps a person can take to help him or her experience release from guilt's grasp.

• Accept personal responsibility for past wrong acts. Also accept by faith the forgiveness given you by God.

• Study and memorize passages of Scripture that testify to God's forgiveness. Build an inner confidence in what God has promised and done for you.

• Recognize that the new life that salvation brings is to be a holy one. Consciously turn away from the sins of the past that brought you guilt. Choose new ways that express your willingness to serve God and live His way.

• Build close relationships with other Christians who give and receive forgiveness and who "spur one another on toward love and good deeds" (10:24). Identifying with the people of God and experiencing their acceptance can help you sense God's acceptance and love and can make forgiveness more real to you.

HABITS

Have you ever noticed? We almost always add the word "bad" when we talk about habits. Even the New Testament, which only mentions habits twice, speaks of "getting into" habits that are far from commendable.

When we look at Daniel's practice of getting down on his knees three times a day to pray (Dan. 6:10), there's no hint this regular action of his was a "habit." Even though he kept the practice up not just for months or years, but decades. What is it that makes "idle talk" (1 Tim. 5:13) a bad habit, but consistent prayer something else?

One difference may lie in the fact that a habit is generally thought of as a more or less automatic response to a situation. It's something you do without thinking. Maybe your habit is taking a second piece of pie with supper. Or an extra spoonful of sugar with your coffee. Maybe it's turning on the TV to watch "Nightline" before going to bed. Or your habit may be gossiping about others when you sit down to lunch with friends. Or honking your horn when other drivers annoy you. What's common with all these illustrations is that a given situation (having coffee, getting ready for bed, etc.) keys a behavior you do without thinking. Almost always those automatic responses we label habits are bad for us: perhaps not as an isolated act, but harmful when they become a regular pattern.

In contrast, good habits (like prayer, or speaking well of others, or eating nonfattening foods) usually call for self-discipline. We have to consciously work at keeping up the good practices; the bad habits call for no effort at all.

So how are bad habits broken? There seem to be two basic approaches.

• The modern approach calls for identifying situations that trigger the automatic responses. If pie on the table leads you to reach for a second piece, make sure the pie is cut and put on the plate in the kitchen. Only small, single helpings should be brought to the table. If gossip always starts at lunch, try eating alone. By avoiding situations that stimulate a habitual response, we may break the habit with a minimum of pain.

• The older approach calls for facing the issue head on and exercising willpower. We look at the situation and understand the real nature of the habit. That extra piece of pie every day means ten added pounds this year, with increased danger of heart attack. We formulate a clear picture of the ideal: we picture ourselves pushing back from the table, losing weight, and getting into those slacks that hang, useless, in the closet. Desiring to realize the ideal, we change our response by serious and persistent practice. The pie is still sitting on the table. But we refuse to reach for that second piece.

I have a notion some of us will be attracted to the second approach. Brave confrontation and reliance on willpower seem more courageous. Actually though, when it comes to bad habits, it seems wise to follow Paul's advice to Timothy. "Flee the evil desires of youth," Paul warned, and "don't have anything to do with foolish and stupid arguments" (2 Tim. 2:22, 23). Avoiding situations in which habit or emotions stimulate an automatic response may be the better part of wisdom.

HAPPINESS

Happiness is an illusive thing. People can tell you when they're happy. But no one has come up with a good definition of what happiness is. Researchers have tried. What have they found? Happiness is *not sexual* satisfaction, a stressless childhood, education, occupation, a person's religious affiliation, or even whether or not an individual is handicapped. While most people in several studies felt money has a lot to do with happiness, the affluent report about the same levels of satisfaction and frustration with life as the rest of us. Even age seems to have little impact. The young claim to want happiness more than other groups. But young adults, middle-aged adults, and older adults report that they achieve about the same degree of happiness.

After surveying some 52,000 readers from ages 15 to 95, *Psychology Today* concluded that "happiness turns out to be more a matter of how you regard your circumstances than of what the circumstances are." The magazine suggested that four attitudes were essential to happiness: a sense of emotional security, a lack of cynicism, the belief that life has meaning, and a sense of personal responsibility for and control of events.

The Bible gives less attention to happiness than we do. Perhaps that is because our common notion of "happiness" tends to focus our attention outward, looking for the things or the circumstances that will "make" us happy. In contrast, Scripture focuses our attention elsewhere as, for instance, in the Beatitudes. You remember the Beatitudes. They are those brief "blessed are" statements in Matthew 5:1–12, that some versions actually translate "happy are." They proclaim the stunning news that the blessed (the "happy") are really the poor in spirit, the meek, those who mourn, and those who are "persecuted because of righteousness." Hardly things most people seek to make them happy!

Why then are these people "blessed"? In part because the future is more important to them than their present, for they know that one day they will experience God's richest blessing. But they are fortunate even now—blessed, and even happy—because in a world searching vainly for "happiness," they are anchored in personal commitment to those values that give life meaning. Because they have discovered God's way to look at circumstances, their happiness can come from deep within.

HOPE

Hope keeps people going. In fact, many psychologists feel that having something to look forward to is what keeps individuals from drifting into despair. Even looking forward to a phone call from a friend or fresh strawberries for breakfast seems to give life some meaning. Picking out something to look forward to tomorrow, or next week, or this summer, helps us keep a positive outlook on our life.

But hope means even more in a Christian context.

Hope spells out our confidence that God is in charge of the future. Tomorrow and eternity are filled with His good gifts, so we face life with confident expectation (cf. 2 Thess. 2:16; 1 Thess. 4:18). No, we don't "hope against hope" for some unlikely lottery win. We look forward to the sure grace and goodness of our loving God.

HUMILITY

Now we know the truth about ourselves. Some researchers in a study have shown that most of us view friends, neighbors, and co-workers as pretty inferior compared with ourselves. And that nearly everyone expects greater than average rewards in pay and praise.

This assumption of our superiority is the opposite of humility. The truly humble don't display false modesty. Instead the humble person accepts his or her own strengths with joy, accepts praise with appreciation, and finds satisfaction in following Paul's advice to the Philippians: "Do nothing out of selfish ambition or vain conceit, but in humility consider others better than yourselves. Each of you should look not only to your own interests, but also to the interests of others. Your attitude should be the same as that of Christ Jesus" (2:3–5).

IDENTITY

"You are all sons of God through faith in Christ Jesus, for all of you who were baptized into Christ have clothed yourselves with Christ. There is neither Jew nor Greek, slave nor free, male nor female, for you are all one in Christ Jesus" (Gal. 3:26–28). This is our identity.

INDIVIDUALITY

A number of terms describe the traits of an individual. Care for a partial list? Well, how about: submissive, acquiescent, ambitious, competitive, aspiring, friendly, good-natured, argumentative, independent, stubborn, resolute, determined, adventurous, deferent, respectful, assertive, decisive, dramatic, timid, cautious, sensitive, shy, nervous, sympathetic, gentle, protective, organized, neat, precise, playful, easy-going, exclusive, aloof, sensuous, sensitive, dependent, helpless, intellectual, curious, logical, creative. . . . And there are many more.

It's good to appreciate the fact that people have differences. We don't want to fall into the trap of viewing Christians as members of some cookie-cutter brigade, all lined up, just alike, surrendering individuality just to fit in. You and I can be ourselves, each with our own differences, and still experience "unity among yourselves as you follow Christ Jesus, so that with one heart and mouth you may glorify the God and Father of our Lord Jesus Christ" (Rom. 15:5, 6).

INTERDEPENDENCE

What does interdependence mean as a practical matter? Attitude. It means respect for others. Consideration for others. Listening to others. Appreciation for what others contribute. Sharing with others. It means living out the conviction that your life and mine have greater meaning when we build close personal relationships in which we give—and receive. "Dependence" suggests a surrendering of one's own personal significance. And "independence" suggests a rejection of close personal relationships; a decision to go it alone. But "interdependence" guards both individuality and relationship.

KNOWING GOD'S WILL

What college shall I go to? Should I move and take that new job? Is this the time to buy that new car? These and many other genuine concerns make us wonder about God's will. We're concerned about it because we believe He wants to guide us in our life-shaping choices. We believe God has a "best" for us (cf. Ps. 32:8). But at the same time, we're confused. How do we come to know God's will? Is there a process through which He guides us to make good choices? Let's begin by understanding that "God's will" is used in at least three senses in the Bible—the principled will, the prophetic will, and the personal will.

• Principled will. In verse 9 of Colossians 1 Paul prays that believers might be "filled with a knowledge of his [God's] will." What is he saying here? His reference is to the fact that God has shared with us in the Scriptures specific principles by which believers are to live. The Scriptures give insight into what is right and wrong, as well as into the values we are to have. The principled will of God is the great body of revealed truths that we are to study and to apply. So the answer to our question, "Is this God's will for me?" can often be found in His principled will. Let's say you've fallen in love with a nonbeliever. All your emotions insist that this is the one. But a look at 2 Corinthians 6:14–16 and 1 Corinthians 7:39 show you God's principled will, and you know that, however much you pray and ask God for a sign, the marriage simply is not His will for you.

Living by God's principled will calls for our full commitment. God will not force us to be obedient, and we can resist. This aspect of God's will focuses responsibility squarely on you and me. When we commit ourselves to obedience we both glorify God and choose paths that lead us to His very best.

• Prophetic will. Some Scriptures tell what God has determined *will* happen, regardless of individual human choices. The best illustration of this is found in prophecy. Over and over in the Old Testament we find God announcing beforehand what will happen. The Babylonians will carry Judah into captivity. The Messiah will be born in Bethlehem and die on a cross. History's march will end with a great tribulation. Jesus will return. These grand announcements of what God has determined rest on the foundation of His sovereign purpose and will come to pass. God's prophetic will does not involve our response, for there is nothing we can do to cooperate or to resist. Revelation of God's prophetic will calls on us to recognize His awesome power and worship Him.

• Personal will. God's personal will is distinctively different from both the principled and prophetic will. We see illustrations of God's personal will in many stories of the Bible.

Abraham's servant was guided to Rebekah as a bride for Isaac (Gen. 24). Isaiah and Jeremiah were called to special ministries, and Amos was led away from his herds to serve as a prophet to Israel. Paul was led to go to Macedonia and then to Jerusalem—against the advice of many friends—where he was imprisoned. In each case, at a turning point in life, God acted to lead these believers into special paths.

While you and I are not Isaiahs or Amoses or Pauls, we are important to God. And His Spirit is present to guide us in the significant decisions of our lives. God does have a personal will for you and me. He will help us find it.

Discerning God's personal will. Again, we're back to the question—when you or I have a significant decision to make, how do we go about it? How does God make that personal will known? There are ways we can be sure God is *not* showing us His will, which we'll call perversions of His will. Another way of exploring God's will is to look into the prerequisites to His will and finally, there may be patterns for discovering God's personal will. But first let's look at perversions of God's will.

Some people treat finding God's will as something magical. But we should not say "If the phone rings in the next 20 minutes, God wants me to. . . ." Nor should we open the Bible with eyes closed, punch our finger at a verse, and call it guidance. We also want to be careful not to ask God's will in trivial matters. God may be interested in what tie you wear tomorrow, but He is quite willing to leave the choice up to you. Many of the daily choices we make have no real consequence in the ultimate scheme of things. We should be willing to take responsibility for all such decisions, exercising good sense and good taste.

The second means of discerning God's will has to do with prerequisites. God has a basic will for non-Christians—to come to know Him. Becoming one of His children is the first step to knowing His will since personal guidance calls for personal relationship. Beyond this, you and I need to approach the search for God's personal will with an attitude of commitment. Willingness to do God's will is basic. Sometimes what we call a desire to know God's will is nothing less than a desperate search for permission to do something we already know is wrong. Obedience is essential to discovering God's will.

Lastly, we should understand that personal guidance does not come magically but is discerned in the overlapping patterns of our lives. The primary pattern is found in Scripture, where God's direct commands and principles help us understand His values. We know, for instance, that sexual immorality is never the will of God no matter what our emotions or temptations (cf. 1 Thess. 4:3; 5:15–18). If we have a choice to make between two jobs, God may impress upon us that one job, more so than the other, gives special opportunity to serve the needy, and in this way we have a pattern to help us decide. Other patterns may involve our skills, our likes and dislikes, what doors are open to us. It would seem unlikely God is calling us to be a doctor if we find study hard or if we hate chemistry. Consider, as well, how the good advice of those who know us provides a pattern or guide for us (cf. Prov. 27:17, 19). As Christians we are members of a body, surrounded by those who know us, our strengths, weaknesses, and gifts. We can share the process of decision making with others and listen to their advice.

How will we really know God's will? There will be no voices from heaven. And when we make our choices, we may not be sure then that what we choose is best. Colossians 3:15 speaks of peace ruling within, acting as an umpire to assure us deep down that we have chosen rightly. If we are experiencing constant turmoil and distress after making a decision, it may mean taking the time to go back and reevaluate, for God may be telling us we've taken a wrong turn.

Just knowing that Jesus lives, we can remain confident that, if we are committed to pleasing Him,

He will guide us. We may not "know" as we make our choice, for our life must be lived by faith, but we can trust Him, the living, loving God.

LISTENING

When we're with other people good listening communicates respect and is a key to close, loving relationships. But being a good listener isn't easy. It calls for concentrated effort and the development of several skills. We can describe good listening as active, reflective, and responsive.

• Active. Sometimes when we're with others we focus on what we're going to say next, not on what they're saying. Active listening focuses on the other person. We are attuned to not only what is said, but the other person's feelings. Tone of voice, a nervous laugh, a tightening of the lips, all can convey information about how the person is feeling. When we want to understand and care, we need to listen not only to what is said but to how it is said.

• Reflective. Reflective listening means we respond to the feelings expressed. We reflect the feelings we think we hear. We don't reflect all the time, of course. But when a friend, who appears stressed, says, "Jim was late again last night," it's appropriate for us to say, "You sound concerned." Our reflective statement may miss the mark. The friend may not be concerned at all but hurt at Jim's thoughtlessness. But on target or off, our attempt to reflect her feelings at least lets her know we're willing to talk about her deeper feelings. We let her know that our concern isn't superficial; we really care about what is going on inside.

• Responsive. Loving relationships are never one-way. If we were to only listen and reflect another's feelings, always on the hearing end and never on the sharing, others become uncomfortable with us. Once we move beyond the superficial, we need to be willing to communicate our own deepest feelings.

The whole process of sensitive listening is deeply embedded in the Bible's description of how we are to live with one another. Caring, sharing, sensitivity, acceptance, bearing of others' burdens—all these are woven through the New Testament's portrait of the Christian community.

LISTENING TO GOD

Listening to others means giving them our full attention and being responsive. If you were to look through a concordance sometime, you would quickly discover that listening to God also implies response. A specific response. Biblically speaking, if you or I fail to *do* what God says, we've neither listened to nor heard Him.

LONELINESS

According to one national study, it seems that within any four- or five-week period more than a quarter of all Americans feel painfully lonely. Surprisingly, people in their late sixties and older are less lonely than adolescents and young adults.

Causes of loneliness. Two kinds of loneliness can be identified: some speak of "loneliness of the inner self" or of "spiritual loneliness," that comes when life seems to have no meaning. But most of us experience loneliness as a kind of sad emotion that comes when we feel separated from others. Some researchers suggest that loneliness is a symptom of changes in society—the breakdown of the family and the mobility of people. Children and young adults are confused by divorce and often experience loneliness. People who are forced to move for their jobs also face lonely circumstances.

Cure of loneliness. All of us are likely to experience loneliness at times. But loneliness need not be a permanent experience. There are hedges against loneliness. One is social attachment. Attachment relationships are those we view as permanent, which provide stability and closeness. While marriage is the primary attachment relationship for most adults, it is not the only one. For some, roommates offer a stable attachment, and many singles have shared households for years. Some believers have their need for a sense of permanent relationship met in God. David expresses this in Psalm 27, sharing his confidence that "though my father and mother forsake me, the LORD will receive me" (27:10). For still others, a ministering relationship fulfills their need for attachment: years invested in caring for children as a foster parent or nurse or working with unwed mothers in a half-way house.

Another hedge against loneliness is found in community, that is, in a network of relationships. Becoming a Christian means entering a relationship with other people as well as with God: a relationship that offers us the possibility of a rich community experience.

The blessing of loneliness. While loneliness would never seem to be a pleasant experience, it may, in fact, be a blessing. It may be God's way of letting us know that we haven't yet experienced all the benefits of our relationship with Him. Loneliness may be God's way of urging us to reach out, to build relationships, to avail ourselves of the richer, fuller life He has in store for us.

LOVE

No one can quite define the nature of love. Romantic love can be wonderful, making us bubble inside. But it can also be painful, particularly if it turns out not to be "genuine" love. Because being in love is such an exciting experience, most of us never stop to wonder if being in love means the same for others as for us. Let us examine different ways people love.

• Beauty love. Some people fall in love with the person whom they find most physically attractive. When they meet someone who approaches their ideal, passion erupts into intense desire. This kind of lover often seeks an immediate sexual relationship. But disappointment is likely to result because they are reaching for an ideal rather than a real person. And a real person will almost always fall short in some way. This relationship will quickly dissolve.

• Love as a game. Some people enjoy playing at love. Courtship is a pleasant pastime, and brief affairs are simply "scores." The person who plays at love doesn't want to become seriously involved and isn't interested in sharing. The player shies away from talk about the future and feels most secure when dating several persons rather than just one.

• Love as affection. Some people love slowly. Their feelings are likely to evolve as a friendship deepens. An exhausting, flitting form of love holds no attraction for these kinds of people. Their goal is a stable, comfortable marriage marked by deepening appreciation and shared enjoyment of the basic things in life.

• Love as obsession. For some, love strikes unexpectedly and against all reason. The obsessive lover may not even particularly like the one he or she loves. They may feel caught, helpless in a "love's" grip.

• Love as shopping. People who "shop" for love simply recognize that marriage and family are an important part of life. This person carefully evaluates the values desired in a mate and goes about looking for likely prospects. Love feelings can grow later. For them, marriage and mate selection are too important to leave to the emotions.

Measuring love. Most of us can make quick and solid value judgments about these ways of loving. Some are clearly selfish: the lover loves only for what he or she gains. Others seem to open the door to something more.

In one sense, romantic love is intended to be selfish. That is, God gave us the capacity and the desire for love. He shaped us so we might experience its mystery, its wonder, and its delight. Each of us is meant to be enriched by loving and by being loved. And yet because loving relationships involve another person, we can't be concerned just about ourselves. Our feelings are important. But if we don't respect the other person's feelings, we risk using those we love.

The Bible's standard of love is unveiled in Christ. It is really more of a "romantic" love than we might realize. Surely *agape* is no cool, impersonal, passionless kind of love. God calls us His precious ones, and His joy wells up as we respond to Him. Like any lover, God is enriched as He cares for us. What sets God apart as the greatest of lovers is His sensitivity to the needs of the beloved and His willingness to give as well as to receive.

MARRIAGE

In these days of "living together" and quick divorce, many young adults question the meaning of marriage. Many question the value of a marriage ceremony. After all, marriage is just a license for sex, some will say, and sex is a private thing. Why involve everyone in an expensive show when the marriage may not even last?

Biblical roots. To understand marriage we have to go back to the ideal established in Scripture. The story told in Genesis 2 is the foundation for our understanding. God created man. Adam had all of Eden to explore, and he delighted in his garden, observing the birds and animals, which he named. But he became increasingly aware of an emptiness, for in all of Eden "no suitable helper was found." But God took a rib from Adam and from it, shaped Eve. The message was not lost on Adam. He recognized when he first saw Eve, that though she differed in form, she was his equal in every way, sharing an identity as one who is made in the image of God. This message echoes in Adam's words: "This is now bone of my bones and flesh of my flesh" (Gen. 2:23). Genesis goes on to say, "for this reason a man will leave his father and mother and be united to his wife, and they will become one flesh" (v. 24).

This passage instituting marriage establishes the ideal. Marriage is a relationship between two individuals who share a common identity, rooted in an equal share of the image of God. Marriage is a helping relationship, designed for the growth and enrichment of each person. Marriage is a "we" relationship, in which the couple learns to live life as a unit (as "one flesh"). Marriage is a relationship between equals, for only equals can become "one." It is only later, with the entrance of sin in human nature, that marriage is distorted into a hierarchy with the husband "ruling over" the wife (Gen. 3:16).

Our problem today with marriage has to do with distortion; we think of marriage as nothing more than licensed sex or as a bondage designed to keep women as slaves to men. Marriage is far more than a license to enjoy sex without guilt, and it is something very different from a way to enslave. Marriage is a lifelong commitment in which each person, as an equal, commits himself or herself to being a helper to the other.

Certain issues have caused problems in marriages, issues like: Should a wife work? Should the husband help with housecleaning? Should a couple move if a better job offer comes for the woman? Every society has its own current notions on the "right" answers to questions like these. And many Christians will have stereotyped ideas about appropriate roles for husbands and wives. But it's important for a couple—and for the Christian community—to recognize that such issues are not essential to a marriage. Each couple must have freedom to work out their own solution and find their own balance. But they must do so in ways that maintain the essence of marriage, which is: a commitment to consider the needs and feelings of each and to arrive at a "we" decision that is best.

The marriage ceremony. Marriage is obviously more than an announcement that two people are going to have sex. Marriage is a public commitment: an announcement to the community that from now on the issues of life will be met by "us," not just by "me." Marriage is a promise that whatever the future may hold—sickness or health, better or worse—the future will be met together, with each individual there to help and support, to love and respect the other. The "I dos" spoken in solemn vows before God, in public, in the light of day, certainly mean far more than any "I love you" whispered in the dark in the back seat of a car. The ceremony is an affirmation of trust. Finally, the ceremony is important to the community because it means that another couple has stood to testify that life holds more than personal gratification, that "we" truly *is* more important than "me." The wedding affirms that God's plan for meeting our deepest needs is the best plan after all.

MATURITY

Prayers for maturity produce unexpected answers. Why? Because maturity comes only through a long, painful process. But James has a comforting thought about this process. He said you can "consider it pure joy, my brothers, whenever you face trials of many kinds, because you know that the testing of your faith develops perseverance. Perseverance must finish its work so that you may be mature and complete, not lacking anything" (1:2–4). So go ahead. Pray for maturity. Welcome your trials. It's worth it all to be complete.

MONEY

Maybe you've puzzled over a particular story Jesus told. It's called the Parable of the Shrewd Manager found in Luke 16. It's about a manager who'd been dipping into company funds. When the owner of the company heard rumors about an auditor appearing, he warned the manager. In panic the manager called in all the company creditors and rewrote the books. A person who had a bill for $20,000 got it cut to $10,000 and another who owed $18,000 got it readjusted to $12,000. The owner later commended the manager for being so shrewd. Jesus' comment was, "For the people of this world are more shrewd in dealing with their own kind than are the people of the light. I tell you, use worldly wealth to gain friends for yourselves, so that when it is gone, you will be welcomed into eternal dwellings" (vv. 8, 9).

What's He saying? Simply this. Let's never be foolish and mistake money as riches. Money is just something to use, to help us prepare for the future. The wise person recognizes this fact and spends his money with the fact of eternity in mind.

"No servant can serve two masters," Jesus concluded. "Either he will hate the one and love the other, or he will be devoted to the one and despise the other. You cannot serve both God and Money" (v. 13).

PAIN

One way to look at pain is to see it as God's early warning system. The flame burns and we jerk our hand back before we can be seriously injured. And in this sense, pain is a gift.

Obviously not all pain comes gift-wrapped. Take chronic pain—the nagging backache that sells so many Doan's pills or the persistent migraine. This kind of pain drains life of all joy. Can this pain too be a gift?

All things, in some way, work together for good in our lives. And God uses even pain to shape us toward Christlikeness (Rom. 8:28, 29). Relief from pain can also be a great gift. So let's focus on healing. Is there relief these days from chronic pain?

Doctors and researchers are finding an increasing number of ways to release us from pain. Pain clinics are becoming relatively common and use any number of techniques: biofeedback, acupuncture, electrical stimulation, hypnosis, drugs, exercise, and other means to deal with the physical roots of our pain. But the evidence mounts that this kind of treatment isn't enough. It's our personal reaction to pain that's proving to be one of the most significant factors for recovery.

All too often pain has its little hidden benefits. A

wife may show extra affection when her husband is in pain, and unconsciously he's willing to suffer a little for that reward. A nagging backache is likely to persist—if it means a person can stay home from a difficult, boring job. The pain is real, but we're less willing to fight to overcome it unless there's some payoff. Studies have shown that people who live exciting, active lives are seldom incapacitated by pain. It's not that people with chronic pain pretend or even that they want the pain, it's just that the overall quality of their lives has a significant impact on recovery.

Look at it this way. Persistent pain may be God's invitation to us to reevaluate our lives. Is returning to our normal life important to us, or is it possible that our "normal life" isn't as full of meaning as God intends it to be? If we suffer chronic pain, it's vital to get medical help, of course. But it may be spiritually vital to look at our life and see if God is urging us to stretch toward something more.

Interestingly, the particular pain most often referred to in the Bible is the pain of childbirth. Out of agony, a fresh new life is born. In the same way, pain may be for the sufferer a prelude to a fresh new life.

PASSION

You can tell a lot about a word by the other words with which it keeps company. For instance, the word "passion" is never associated with words like "mild" or "calm." Instead "passion" always seems to hang around with "overwhelming," "towering," and "ungovernable."

And passion is usually associated with sex. While it certainly can be used to describe ardent love and sexual desire, passion actually describes emotions of every sort, as distinct from reason. The phrase "distinct from reason" is important. We never expect anyone "in the grip of passion" to stop to think or to be reasonable. Passion demands impulsive action.

A quick glance in the Bible suggests that passion isn't a very respectable word. Not that emotions and feelings are wrong. But the New Testament Epistles view the roots of passion as sunk deep in the old nature. Galatians 5:24 speaks of "the sinful nature with its passions," and Titus 2:12 and 3:3 mention both "ungodliness and worldly passions" and being "enslaved by all kinds of passions." The key word associated with passion here is enslaved. Whenever any emotion grips us so strongly that we're overpowered by it, we've lost our way. No wonder God says the passions that grip us are in conflict with the Spirit.

So next time you feel your passions aroused, stop and do this simple check. That same Galatians passage tells us that the fruit produced when the Spirit is in control is "love, joy, peace, patience, kindness, goodness, faithfulness, gentleness and self-control" (Gal. 5:22). If the passion you're experiencing is not associated with goodness, then it had better be abandoned.

POTENTIAL

"I could be a writer . . ." an acquaintance used to tell me. I agreed. I never question anyone's claim to have potential. I know that God made us wonderfully and well: tremendous potential is part of what it means to be a human being and redeemed.

But my acquaintance, who is sure she could write, has not and probably never will. Jesus' familiar story of the talents illustrates why. Each received a different treasure entrusted to him and was told to invest it. Each who did so was praised: he had been faithful in using what he had. The individual who wrapped his talent and buried it took no risks. And he won no praise.

It's not our potential that counts. It's what we do with it that concerns God.

PRAYER

Too many books on prayer approach it as if it were an obstacle course. God's answer is a prize to be won but only if we overcome hurdles He's placed in our way. Only if we use just the "right technique"— believing when we ask, not regarding sin in our hearts, asking God's will, not having selfish motives, and so on.

This concept of prayer distorts the image we are

given in the Bible of a loving, welcoming God. The God who invites us to come to Him in prayer is the warm, loving Father we know so well in Jesus—not some distant Judge who is more concerned with our technique than with our need. These three New Testament passages convey the approachable nature of God.

• "We do not have a high priest who is unable to sympathize with our weaknesses, but we have one who has been tempted in every way, just as we are—yet was without sin. Let us then approach the throne of grace with confidence, so that we may receive mercy and find grace to help us in our time of need" (Heb. 4:15, 16).

• "And when you pray, do not keep on babbling like pagans, for they think they will be heard because of their many words. Do not be like them, for your Father knows what you need before you ask him. This, then, is how you should pray: Our Father . . ." (Matt. 6:7–9).

• "Ask and it will be given to you; seek and you will find; knock and the door will be opened to you. For everyone who asks receives; he who seeks finds; and to him who knocks, the door will be opened. Which of you, if his son asks for bread, will give him a stone? Or if he asks for a fish, will give him a snake? If you, then, though you are evil, know how to give good gifts to your children, how much more will your Father in heaven give good gifts to those who ask him!" (Matt. 7:7–11).

To understand prayer, we simply need to consider the character of our God. We need to see the loving Father. We need to hear Him invite us to share every need and confess every sin. Prayer is not "spiritual exercise," not an obstacle course, not a religious duty. It is nothing less than responding to the warm assurance of God's love.

PRIORITIES

We all know priorities are important. And actually, it's quite easy to set them. Just follow these simple steps:

1. Make a list of the things you commonly do each day, or week.
2. Jot down beside each item the amount of time you typically spend daily or weekly.
3. Put a check mark beside "must" activities and place a plus mark beside three "most important" activities.
   Put a minus mark beside three "least important" activities.
4. Write down your three most important personal relationships.

Now, look over the list with its times, checks, pluses, and minuses, and underline activities that specifically enrich the three important personal relationships you identified.

In setting priorities, time is the key. That check list should give you guidance, helping you see where you can rearrange your use of time to focus more on the relationships or things that are important to you.

Putting this kind of evaluation down on paper is important. But it won't make any real difference until you engrave those priorities deeply in your heart and life.

PURPOSE

"I press on to take hold of that for which Christ Jesus took hold of me. Brothers, I do not consider myself yet to have taken hold of it. But one thing I do: Forgetting what is behind and straining toward what is ahead, I press on toward the goal to win the prize for which God has called me heavenward in Christ Jesus. All of us who are mature should take such a view of things" (Phil. 3:12–15).

RELAX!

Imagine yourself floating in a canoe on the surface of a calm northern lake. You feel the sun warming you; you hear the clear waters lap calmly against the side of the canoe. You hear the distant cry of the loon. Feel relaxed?

The problem is, we can't spend our whole life laid

back. Our daily lives are pressure-packed. And it's how we handle the daily pressures that make so many people tense and worried.

But Christians do have the advantage in handling pressures. We don't all use it, but that extra edge is ours if we want it. You see, we can live with pressures but without anxiety. How? The Book of Hebrews promises us that we can enter God's rest (4:1–11). The writer explains that God's own work "has been finished since the creation of the world." He is not saying God is inactive. Instead he points out that nothing can happen in the whole course of history for which God is not prepared. The Creation takes every possibility into action. Thus there is no problem you or I can face for which God has not already worked out the solution.

Why then do we worry? God knows the way through our wilderness; all we need to do is follow.

When we grasp this great truth and trust our problems to the Lord, we find rest. We turn from reliance on our own efforts (Heb. 4:10) and find the wonderful freedom to relax.

REPENTANCE

Repentance is more than a cheap "I'm sorry" or a moment of sorrow. Repentance is always associated with the choice of a new direction for life.

When repentance is real, there is a change of lords: Jesus replaces even the most inviting sins. There is a new outlook and life has a new objective: we learn to live to please God.

This understanding of the Bible's radical view of repentance isn't something to use as a weapon against others. We don't say, "If you were *really* sorry, you'd . . ." Words on repentance are God's personal message to us. Do we know Him in such a deep and true way that our repentance is a sincere act? Paul says it this way: "Examine yourselves to see whether you are in the faith" (2 Cor. 13:5).

RESOLUTIONS

Are those New Year's resolutions we make or the promises we make to ourselves to watch our diet helpful or harmful? Should we make resolutions? Or are they like promises made to God that only make us more guilty when we break them?

Resolutions can be good for us. We need to set personal goals and to try to reach them. But part of our confusion arises when we look back and see our past littered with shattered resolutions. It makes us feel helpless, guilty, even ashamed. What must God think of us?

We can know what God thinks of us from the Bible. He knows us and remembers we are dust (Ps. 103:14). He knows our temptations and is able to sympathize with our weaknesses (Heb. 4:15). He understands and reaches down to help us up whenever we fall. Resolutions are good, as long as we are as willing to forgive ourselves when we stumble, as God is, and are willing to get up and try again.

RESPONSIBILITY

It boils down to just one thing: Do I face the fact that *I choose* to do and to be what I am? Blaming others or fate may seem to offer an easy way out. But the fact is that each of us bears personal responsibility for our every act. Galatians 6 sums up the Bible's teaching succinctly. "A man reaps what he sows. The one who sows to please his sinful nature, from that nature will reap destruction; the one who sows to please the Spirit, from the Spirit will reap eternal life (vv. 7b–8)."

It's good to know that God gives us freedom to choose. And that when we choose life in the Spirit, He adds this promise: "At the proper time we will reap a harvest if we do not give up (v.9)."

RIGHTS

We all have rights and want to keep them. It's no wonder some people bristle when they feel someone is infringing on their rights. Our fiercely protective attitude toward personal rights is certainly one of the basic causes of conflict.

Scripture does not suggest that individuals have no rights. The Bible never even hints that it's all right for you or me to trample on the rights of others. What the Bible does do, in the New Testament, is ask us to stop and think a moment before insisting on our own rights.

Three passages are particularly instructive. In 1 Corinthians 9:12 Paul speaks of his own right to be supported financially by those to whom he ministers. Yet he says, "We did not use this right." He wanted to model in his own life the fact that the gospel is a free gift.

In 1 Corinthians 10 Paul writes to people who believed they had a right to eat meat sacrificed by pagans in their temples. Paul didn't deny them that right, but he points out that while everything may be permissible, "not everything is beneficial. 'Everything is permissible'—but not everything is constructive. Nobody should seek his own good, but the good of others" (vv. 23, 24).

In Romans a similar conflict developed over whether it was right or wrong to eat temple market meat. The meat eaters had their rights. But Paul says, "If your brother is distressed because of what you eat, you are no longer acting in love" (14:15).

The point is simple but profound. We have rights—but our rights are never more important than the people among whom God has placed us. People of the world may fight for their rights. But the Christian has the privilege of choosing to give up personal rights, in the interest of love.

SALVATION

I wonder. How many signs and billboards in the United States announce "Jesus Saves" or quote "Believe on the Lord Jesus Christ and thou shalt be saved?" I've seen them painted on barns, lettered crudely on home-made signs along roads, and shining in bright neon over rescue mission doors. I'm certainly not against them. Still, I wonder. What does that word "saved" mean to those who pass by? For that matter, what does it mean to us?

God's Old Testament people had a pretty clear idea of salvation. Old Testament references reflect the quiet conviction that God acted in history to help His people. "Saved" was full of meaning. It expressed the belief of the Israelites that God Himself acted to deliver . . . from sickness, from the wicked, from troubles, and from the threat of death. Every foe, whether physical or spiritual, had to surrender to the power of God. Salvation was an exciting word then. Human beings might be weak, but God was great and willing to help.

In the New Testament "salvation" refers in depth to spiritual deliverance. It is not only the external enemy from whom human beings need rescue, but the enemy within—the guilt of past sins and the urge to continue sinning. The New Testament trumpets the good news: God who acted in history also acts within man. Because of Jesus individuals have been saved, are being saved, and will be saved.

The use of these different tenses in the New Testament tells us that when God acts to meet our spiritual needs, He is completely thorough. That we *have been* saved, speaks of the fact that through Christ's death our sins are forgiven. There is no more guilt, because our sins are gone. The past is no longer held against us, for Jesus has worked a startling miracle and wiped out our past wrongs (Heb. 10:17, 18).

We *are being* saved, speaks of the fact that the living Jesus is with us, to lend His own resurrection power to break the grip sin has over us. Because God acts within us, we can now begin to do good. It is present-tense salvation that Paul writes of to the Philippians: "continue to work out your salvation with fear and trembling." We may find life a struggle. But we know that "it is God who works in you to will and to act according to his good purpose" (Phil. 2:12, 13).

And finally, that we *will be* saved speaks of the fact that in the future, at the Resurrection, the last stain of sin will be cleansed from our personalities. We will then be like God in unblemished purity (Eph. 5:27).

When we put the message of the two testaments together, we have a full and stunning picture of what that word "saved" means. It means that God has chosen to become fully involved, willing and able to meet our every need. God acts to deliver us from dangers both inside and outside of our beings. We are weak. But God is great.

SELF-CONCEPT

How do you view yourself? Do you feel strong and talented? Or do you feel weak and inadequate? If your feelings about yourself are positive, you've got what psychologists call a "good self-image." If they're negative, you're saddled with a "poor self-image."

What's important about our self-concept is that we tend to act in accord with how we see ourselves. If we feel good about ourselves and our abilities, we're likely to move ahead confidently, willing to take on new challenges. If we're gripped by feelings of inadequacy, we may *want* to do well but will fear to try.

Spiritually speaking, both approaches to life are booby-trapped. The person with a good self-image may move out and act but rely on his own abilities rather than on God. Yet Jesus reminds us that in the spiritual realm, "apart from me you can do nothing" (John 15:5). The person with a poor self-image, who fears to try, forgets the great truth that "I can do everything through him who gives me strength" (Phil. 4:13).

What's important for the Christian? We are to build new self-concepts that are in harmony with who God says we are. In a paraphrase of 1 Peter 1:22 and 23 we are informed that we are "not mere mortals now, for the live, permanent word of God has given us his own indestructible heredity." In Christ, God lifts us beyond our old selves, to make possible a vibrant new life in which Jesus Himself enables us to be and do good. When we learn to see ourselves as God says we are, we find the courage to live by faith. We can step out boldly to meet life's challenges, not relying on our own strength but on the empowering presence of our God. We are new creations, reshaped by God's wonderful saving power.

SELF-RIGHTEOUSNESS

You remember the story of the two men at prayer. One was a Pharisee, zealously religious. He glanced contemptuously at his fellow worshiper and then reminded God of all the religious duties he had performed. The other man, well known for his failings, would not even look up to heaven but simply cried out for mercy. Jesus concluded the story by saying, "I tell you that this man, rather than the other, went home justified before God" (Luke 18:14).

Why did Jesus tell this curious little story? He told it for the benefit of listeners "who were confident of their own righteousness and looked down on everybody else" (18:9). This phrase gives us the world's best description of self-righteousness: confidence of one's own righteousness; looking down on everyone else. The story also shows us the danger of self-righteousness. Self-righteousness cuts us off from God's mercy and from other people.

The cure for self-righteousness is God's announcement that "all have sinned and fallen short." This should cause us all to approach God for mercy, to look around at other human beings and realize that we are like them, not better than anyone else. When we abandon our self-righteousness we open ourselves to a healthier personal relationship with God and other human beings.

SENSITIVITY

One psychologist recently observed, "Blessed are the Insensitive Slobs." He meant that life would be easier if we couldn't be hurt. More marriages might hold together, and more parents and children would suffer less from anger and pain. If we were insensitive, how much easier it would seem to do the right thing, never worrying about the possibility of rejection or ridicule from others.

Of course, God has a different idea about sensitivity. As usual. He would want us to become, not less sensitive, but more so. The more tender we are, the more He provides us with His own matchless willingness to forgive. We are all sure to hurt and to be hurt. But the wonderful discovery we make is that it is the healing and not the absence of hurts that binds us closer to others and to God.

SEX

Sex is one of God's finer inventions. He designed us with the capacity to enjoy every sensation and every thrill. And He reassures us in Scripture that intercourse is a gift that enriches our lives.

Of course, we may not use the gift wisely. All too often we want to unwrap the package hastily, before its time. Or we fail to read the directions that tell us how the present is to be assembled. It's likely that most Christians don't even grasp the purpose of sex.

So let's sort through common notions about sex to better understand this gift of God's. We want to handle sex with care, so it will enrich us rather than bring us heartbreak.

The common notion that sex is natural, and therefore right. This is the popular playboy view. Like hunger and thirst, sex is simply a physical thing: a need. This view makes sex something like a ham sandwich or a coke. When you're hungry, you eat. When you're thirsty, you drink. When you're sexually excited, you find someone and jump into bed.

There's no doubt that the sex drive is powerful. This is why Paul points out that in marriage each partner belongs to the other and neither is to withhold his or her body from the other (1 Cor. 7:1–5). But the argument that because the drive exists and is "natural" promiscuous sex is justified, well, it just won't wash. For one thing, there's a difference between our "natural" desire for food and water and our "natural" desire for sex. You can't survive without food and water. Try going without sex for months or even years and you make the stunning discovery that chastity won't kill you! So sex hardly belongs on the same list with those needs that keep us alive.

The common notion that sex is an expression of love and therefore love makes it right. This view has captured the allegiance of many Christians. Sex is *the* way to show love. The problem is, it's a short step from this conviction to the belief that "since we love each other" premarital sex is both good and right. But what do we really mean when we say "love"? Everyone knows that "I love you" can mean "I'm excited by your presence and want you," or it can mean "I care about you as a person and want the best for you." If we mean the first, we're using "love" as a synonym for sexual desire, which never makes anything right. And if we mean the second, it's hard to see how we'd engage in extramarital sex. If we really care for another and want only the best for that person, then the "I love you" won't lead to sex, because we won't risk harming a person we care deeply about.

Actually, the basic notion that having sex is how you show love is just not valid. Think about that for a moment. There are many people each of us loves, and we show that love in many ways. There's shared laughter, long conversations, hugs and caresses, helping, listening, giving support. And no one imagines that loving those who are closest to us needs to find expression in sex. Somehow it takes something more than "love" to make sex the right and good and beneficial gift God intends it to be.

The uncommon notion that sex is the sign and seal of commitment. Sexual experiences are associated with feelings of love. But the heart and soul of the meaning of sex is found in its power to give ultimate expression to our complete, total commitment to another person. Sexual intercourse, expressing as it does full exposure of ourselves to another and the physical joining of two as one, affirms and reaffirms commitment.

This is why marriage is the only context in which sex can be good or right. God has planned that a man and a woman should one day commit themselves before Him and others to face life together as one, till death do they part. In the context of marriage sex takes on a sacramental character, meeting physical needs, expressing love, but more than that, reaffirming oneness. Sex within marriage is intended to say that, in every way, a couple fully trust each other.

The tragedy of modern society and of the Christian misunderstanding of sex is that this deep meaning of intercourse has been lost and the wonder of its potential for fulfillment misplaced. Sex as a natural desire makes it merely a function. Sex as expression of affection is superficial. But sex as the sign and seal of life-long commitment can become richer, fuller, and deeper as the years go by, bonding ever closer two individuals whose lives in every sense are becoming one.

SIN

It's relatively easy to deal with the topic of sin theologically. Massive volumes have been written on sin; a subject theologians call *hamartiology*. Summarized, the main themes are:

• Sin's character. Two groups of Old Testament and New Testament words describe sin as (a) falling short or as (b) rebelling. Inability to live up to what we acknowledge to be good is one aspect of sin: unwillingness to choose the good, thus actively choosing what we know to be wrong, is another.

• Sin's impact. We might note three things here. (a) Acts of sin are violations of God's or human standards and bring us a burden of guilt. We are responsible for our choices and deserve to be punished. (b) The "sin nature" refers to the twisting of human motivations and will, so that every person descended from the first pair has had warped personalities. Our inner unresponsiveness to God is matched by a pull toward wrong-doing, so that without God's help we struggle unsuccessfully to do right even when we want to. (c) Injustice and oppression represent sin institutionalized. It is not only the individual who is affected by sin, but society as a whole.

We all struggle against the pull toward what we know is wrong and then are burdened with the guilt that comes when we fall short or rebel. We all look around us and hurt for our fellow human beings, seeing the wars, the crime, the discrimination, and the economic brutality. But the good news for us is in the discovery that once we've faced the fact that we all suffer from the disease of sin, God wants us to turn to Him for the cure.

So the greatest Bible words associated with sin aren't terms like "rebellion" or "falling short" or "guilt." The greatest words in the Bible are words like "confession," "forgiveness," "new birth," and "salvation." These great Bible words assure us that in Christ, God provides remission of guilt, power to choose against the pull of the desire to sin, and ultimately, cleansing of the very presence of sin.

SINGLENESS

For some it seems the "fate worse than death." But attitudes—and our experiences—seem to be changing. For instance, in 1975, 40.3% of the women between the ages of 20–24 remained single and also 13.8% of those between 25–29. For men the figures were 59.9% and 22.3% respectively. Add to these who have never been married the increasing number of widowed and divorced people, and we find that a significant number of Americans are living single lives.

But it is not easy being single. It's hard, of course, when parents and others insist we *ought* to be married. It's even harder when we feel a little guilty or perhaps ashamed for not fitting in with what society expects.

While there are advantages and disadvantages to both states, the primary advantage perceived by most is that the single person has a flexibility and potential for making choices denied those who live within the necessary restrictions of marriage.

Biblically. In Old Testament times the society and economy were structured around families and marriage was expected. But looking into the New Testament, Paul gives a word of testimony for singleness. "Now to the unmarried and widows I say: It is good for them to stay unmarried, as I am" (1 Cor. 7:8). Later Paul explains. When a person is married he or she is, rightly, concerned with spouse and family. "His interests are divided." But a single person is free to consider only the Lord: his or her "aim is to be devoted to the Lord in both body and spirit" (1 Cor. 7:32–35). The freedom that Paul emphasizes is important because the single person can shape his or her own life, giving undivided devotion to the Lord. And as a Christian and a member of the family of God, the single person can find in brothers and sisters the acceptance, intimacy, and support he or she might otherwise find in a spouse.

There is, of course, the issue of sex. In our society singleness does not mean sexual inactivity. But for Christians who realize that God's one context for intercourse is marriage, singleness raises the issue of celibacy. Paul's advice in this area is valuable. He commends singleness. But points out that if "they cannot control themselves [sexually], they should marry, for it is better to marry than to burn with passion" (1 Cor. 7:9).

Paul's conclusion is one we must reach too. Some are given the gift of living a meaningful, fulfilling

single life. Some are given the gift of living a meaningful, fulfilling married life. Neither condition is "right"
for everyone or even "better" for everyone. Your gift,
whether to live as a single or as a married person,
makes that state God's best for you.

SUCCESS

Everyone has noticed that "success" in our
society is usually measured by the dollar bill. But
success means different things to different people. The
bottom line is certainly different for the artist than the
businessman. But we can't help realizing that even in
religious circles, size and dollars count. How big is
your church? What's your budget? How much for
missions? How many converts or new members this
year?

I don't imagine we'll ever get away from such
notions until Jesus comes, when we appear before Him
and hear Him commend: "Well done, good and faithful
servant!" (Matt. 25:21, 23). Perhaps then we'll realize
that to God, success isn't measured in results, but in
faithfulness.

SUFFERING

The existence of suffering in a universe shaped by a loving, all–powerful God has always troubled people. And there doesn't seem to be an easy answer to the problem. We can observe that suffering and evil are related to human sin, and we can continue to believe that God is able to bring good out of suffering in the believer's life. And yet we mustn't ignore the fact that permitting human suffering was no easy thing for God. In Christ God entered our world to suffer with us and for us. He suffered in an ultimate way we may not even be able to understand until we are in eternity.

When we suffer. Each of us will face personal suffering. And we will wonder: Why? What have I done? Is God punishing me? Is there anything I can do to find release?

Jesus made it clear that human beings will suffer (cf. John 15:18–27). Romans 8:17 suggests that people must suffer. Peter refers to the reaction people have when suffering comes: "Do not be surprised," he says, "at the painful trial you are suffering" (1 Peter 4:12).

Perhaps the most helpful passage in Scripture on suffering is also found in Peter's first letter. There he reminds us that God is watching over us: He guards us as we continue to do good (1 Peter 3:8–12). Peter also talks about the kind of suffering when "you should suffer for what is right" and makes the startling remark that "you are blessed" (3:14). This is far different from corrective suffering, which comes when we willfully choose to sin. Peter also shows how to respond when suffering comes for which we are not to blame. What is his prescription?

• Do not be terrified (3:14). Suffering is not a sign that life is out of control.

• Set apart Christ as Lord (3:15). Remember that Jesus is still in control and trust Him as Lord.

• Maintain a positive outlook (3:15). Others will be amazed, but you can explain the basis of your hope: not the circumstances, but the conviction that Jesus, who loves you, is still at work.

• Keep a clear conscience (3:16). Don't panic into doing wrong but continue your commitment to good behavior.

Peter also points out a reassuring truth. He explains how we can be confident that suffering leads to blessing. He turns our attention to Jesus (3:18), reminding us how He, who did only good, suffered on the cross—not the evil men who betrayed and condemned Him. But His suffering was not purposeless: through it Jesus provides the way for us to God, and He is now at "God's right hand—with angels, authorities and powers in submission to him" (3:22). Jesus' suffering was intended to bring good for others and to bring His own glorification.

Peter's encouragement to us is clear. We may not understand how, but we can be sure that when we suffer, God intends to use our experience to enrich others and to reap a blessing for ourselves.

TEMPTATION

Somehow we've gotten the peculiar idea that temptations are terrible things. Certainly struggling against temptation isn't on anyone's list of fun things to do. But temptations aren't really *bad*.

Remember Adam and Eve. God placed this special tree in Eden and told the first pair not to eat its fruit. Why? It wasn't a trap, if that's what you've been taught. God wasn't hiding in nearby bushes, waiting to pounce when one or the other succumbed to the temptation to try the fruit. Actually, the tree was important for another reason. You see, God determined that human beings would be special. Having been created in His own image, these new living beings would be able to love, to think, to create, to relate . . . and to choose.

That's the significance of the tree. To be like God, humanity must have the chance to choose between good and evil.

Adam and Eve must have been tempted many times as they strolled hand in hand in the garden. The fruit seemed good for food and looked tasty. They often must have exercised their ability to choose and turned away. Finally, picking a moment when the pair was separated, Satan confused Eve. And she used her freedom and made the wrong choice.

But the tree was a good gift, not a trap. It provided an opportunity to choose the right and become stronger, as well as an opportunity to choose the wrong and grow weak.

How then are we to view our temptations? Are they fearful things, forcing us into a struggle we are sure to lose? And is God determined to catch us? Or are temptations a fresh opportunity to choose good; a fresh occasion for overcoming through the strengthening love of God. Temptations are serious. But they are not *bad*. When we choose the right, we discover they are God's good gifts to us.

The anatomy of temptation. James assures us that temptations are not evils brought on us by God. He explains that "God cannot be tempted by evil, nor does he tempt anyone" (1:13). So the problem with temptation lies within ourselves. "Each one is tempted when, by his own evil desire, he is dragged away and enticed" (1:14).

God gives us only "good and perfect" gifts (1:17). In fact, both Paul and the writer of the letter to the Hebrews talk about the gifts God has given us to help us with temptation. God always offers us a way of escape (1 Cor. 10:13), and God always gives us sympathetic understanding and help (Heb. 4:15, 16). Jesus experienced temptation without ever choosing sin. And because He was human He understands our weaknesses. When we turn to Him, He provides "grace to help in time of need."

Overcoming temptation. Jesus' own experience with temptation, reported in the Gospels of Matthew and Luke, provides a model for dealing with our temptations. Matthew 4 and Luke 4 both portray Jesus turning to Scripture for specific guidance. His use of Scripture was far from magical. He simply recalled guiding principles and chose to act on them. Like Jesus, we are given the wonderful privilege of choosing to listen to His voice and to obey.

TRUTH

In Robert Louis Stevenson's *Kidnapped* there is a description of the young hero on a winding stone stairway without a candle. He is told he is to sleep in the room at the top. The youngster stumbles upward in the pitch dark, his hand against the rough-hewn wall. He comes to the upper landing, and just as he is about to step through the door, a flash of lightning illumines empty space beyond the threshold. The uncle, fearful of the boy's claim on the estate, had intended for him to be dashed to death on hidden rocks below the opened door.

The scene Stevenson describes helps us understand the meaning of the biblical term, Truth. Like the flash of lightning, the Word of God unveils the hidden realities of the dark world through which we stumble. Through the Word we come to know that which we could never have discovered on our own.

And God's Truth not only leads us to safety but to freedom. Walking in the light, we discover we are free: free ultimately from all that hurts because we are free to experience all that helps. When we live the Truth, we become disciples of our Lord.

UNDERSTANDING YOUR BIBLE

The Bible is a book of revelation: a message from God delivered in human language. It's intended to be understood and to give guidance. While the Bible is rich and complex, it is *not* difficult to interpret. The Bible is God's Word to common men, not a puzzle to be unraveled only by theologians.

How then do you and I go about understanding the Bible so we will be able to experience God's guidance? Here are simple steps you can take to improve your understanding of the Bible.

Get a good modern version. There are many translations and paraphrases of the Bible in English. Paraphrases (like *Living Letters* or the *Good News* version) are attempts to capture the sense of the original Bible, and translations are more careful attempts to render the original words. Paraphrases may be interesting to read, but they involve too much interpretation to be used as a basic study text. Probably the best current translation is the New International Version (NIV). This accurate and readable translation is a text you can trust as your basic study Bible.

Get an inexpensive Bible handbook. There are many kinds of literature in the Bible. Its 66 books are written against the background of changing historical settings. A good Bible handbook will give you an overview of every paragraph in every book of the Bible and will help you understand the setting and theme of each book. This kind of information is very helpful in determining what is directly applicable to us in our day.

I'm partial to the *Word Bible Handbook,* published in 1982, because it gives paragraph by paragraph orientation. And because I wrote it.

Read to understand and then listen. Before we can apply a particular Bible teaching to our life, we need to understand what God is saying. Too often Christians take a verse out of context and treat it as God's guidance for them. Understanding the Bible isn't a magical process. It calls for us to master the who, what, when, where, and why of a Scripture passage and *then* see how it applies to us.

The simplest and best approach is to read a paragraph carefully and then jot down a sentence or two about what it teaches. When we have a number of sentences summarizing a sequence of paragraphs, we're able to trace the thought [or argument] of a chapter or section. We can then go back and look at specific verses, to understand them in their context. (A good Bible handbook summarizes the argument for you.)

To "listen" to the Bible is to ask yourself, "What does this paragraph or verse mean *for me?*" In this way, we can search for insights into our own experiences, feelings, decisions, and relationships as we are learning to better understand who God is.

Read ready to obey. Many images in the Bible make it clear that we are to respond to what we read. Scripture, the psalmist says, is a light to our path. The picture is of an individual walking through the night, holding a glowing lamp that gives enough light for the next step. As we study the Bible and apply what we learn to ourselves, God shows us how to take our next step. And it is important that we be obedient. It is only as we act on what God shows us in Scripture that we experience the benefit of God's Word in our lives.

Read with regularity. To understand our Bible we need to read it regularly. As we spend time daily in God's Word, learning to recognize God's thoughts and values, and listening daily for His guidance, we are gradually reshaped and transformed. The Bible is not simply a book to turn to in a crisis. It is a book upon which to build our whole lives. You and I can come to the Word with a great sense of joy because we will meet God and because we will grow and be transformed.

Yes, the Bible is a book that *you* can understand.

UNSAVED LOVED ONES

Many of us are continually concerned about unsaved family and friends. We are not sure just how to pray for them. We're even more uncertain about how we can communicate our faith effectively. What biblical principles can guide us?

"You and your house." Paul told a Philippian jailer, "Believe in the Lord Jesus, and you will be saved." Then he added, "and your household" (Acts 16:31). Some Christians have latched onto this statement, believing it expresses God's commitment to bring the family members of believers to salvation. Others interpret it as stating the universality of the gospel offer, noting that in the next verse Paul tells the

Good News about Jesus to the jailer and "all the others in his house." We should realize too that "household" in New Testament times did not mean only "family" but included slaves, servants, and employees.

Yet it is clear that members of believers' families do have a unique opportunity to come to know God. God has shown a special goodness to family members by placing a believer among them to share the gospel and reveal God's grace.

Praying for family. Sometimes concerned believers are uncertain as to how to pray for their family. They will pray with faith but don't know how confident they can be that their loved ones will be saved. This hesitation is due in part to thinking that there are certain "conditions" that must be met before prayers can be answered. But the wonderful truth about prayer is not that we "do it right" but that God "wants all men to be saved and to come to a knowledge of the truth" (1 Tim. 2:4). Praying for our loved ones is never out of the will of God. We can pray in fullest confidence that our request is in harmony with God's own desire.

Witnessing to family. It's often hardest to witness to parents, spouses, and children. Even when our relationship is ideal, telling about Jesus and our new experience with Him may create doubt, ridicule, or even resentment. Unfortunately it seems that intimacy often has its own barriers. In such cases, aggressive witnessing may do more harm than good.

This thought is behind Peter's instruction to wives in his first letter: "Wives, in the same way be submissive to your husbands so that, if any of them do not believe the word, they may be won over without words by the behavior of their wives, when they see the purity and reverence of your lives" (3:1, 2). At times, the gospel is better communicated without words, rather by showing love and responsiveness.

New Testament passages reveal that evangelism should always be gentle and loving. Even in the face of open opposition, "the Lord's servant must not quarrel; instead, he must be kind to everyone, able to teach, not resentful. Those who oppose him he must gently instruct, in the hope that God will grant them repentance leading to a knowledge of the truth" (2 Tim. 2:24, 25). What might we suggest as specific guidelines for witnessing to unsaved loved ones?

• Pray regularly that God's Spirit will open their hearts to the gospel. Pray with confidence, knowing that God loves your loved ones even more than you do.

• Pay attention to the quality of your relationship with your loved ones. Seek to be an even better child, husband, or wife. Let your own life be a testimony to the fact that Jesus enriches relationships. Be a living advertisement for the faith you want another to accept.

• Talk naturally about your faith and experiences without pressuring your loved one to make a commitment. It is important to protect a loved one's sense of freedom to make his or her own choice, without coercion.

• Form a fellowship with others who have unsaved loved ones to pray together and encourage one another.

• Don't have expectations, and don't set a time limit. God will work in His own time. He may desire that your quiet, faithful loving and sharing continue for years before any response comes.

• Encourage yourself with passages like Hebrews 10:35, 36. "Do not throw away your confidence; it will be richly rewarded. You need to persevere so that when you have done the will of God, you will receive what he has promised."

WEAKNESS

Weaknesses are only a problem when we try to hide them from ourselves or others. At least, that's the point of view taken by the apostle Paul, who discovered that weakness can actually be beneficial. In 2 Corinthians 12 Paul reports what God had informed him about weakness, "My grace is sufficient for you, for my power is made perfect in weakness." And Paul describes his experience being weak, "Therefore I will boast all the more gladly about my weaknesses, so that Christ's power may rest on me. That is why, for Christ's sake, I delight in weaknesses, in insults, in hardships, in persecutions, in difficulties. For when I am weak, then I am strong" (vv. 9, 10).

How foolish it is then to pretend about our weaknesses, to struggle alone—when we can rely on Jesus' own perfecting power.

WORK

In a survey taken in the late seventies more than one in four American workers (27%) "felt so ashamed of the quality of the products they were producing that they would not want to buy them themselves." The recession of the early eighties may have halted or reversed the trend. But more emphasis is given to "humanizing" work.

What is "humanizing" work? Basically the phrase has come to indicate that a job should be designed so that it (1) does not damage, degrade, or consistently bore the worker; (2) will be interesting and satisfying; (3) will utilize the skills the worker has and provide opportunities to acquire new skills; (4) will leave unimpaired the worker's ability to function as spouse, parent, citizen, and friend; and (5) will pay a wage that enables the worker to live a "comfortable life." These are fine goals. They do help us realize that any employer is responsible to an employee for more than his or her wages. But in focusing on job conditions, we take our attention away from the meaning of work and from our own attitudes toward our work.

Work as a ministry. This is one of the first considerations from a Christian point of view. Every job (even slavery in New Testament days) provided an opportunity to serve others in some way. The person on the assembly line in Detroit isn't just building cars: he or she is serving the buyer by providing safe transportation. The job may be boring. But viewed as ministry, it is lifted beyond meaningless repetition. Garbage collecting, even when upgraded by the label "sanitation engineer," is hardly an occupation that "utilizes the skills the worker has and provides opportunities to acquire new skills." But this work is essential—a ministry to individuals and the whole community. Work viewed as a ministry makes a difference. For doing our jobs well becomes a significant way of serving Jesus Christ (Eph. 6:7).

Work as source of autonomy and responsibility. The New Testament is very clear that all who are able to make a living should work, rather than remain idle and live off others (2 Thess. 3:6–13). From the beginning God provided work as a vital gift, enabling each person to maintain self-respect (cf. Gen. 2:15).

Work as a means for gaining riches. This theme has historically been associated with the Protestant work ethic. It reflects the notion that God will bless those who do good with material riches. But this idea is not reflected in the New Testament. Ephesians 4:28 presents work as both "useful" (e.g., a ministry) and as a way to earn money "that he may have something to share with those in need." In fact, Timothy is warned that "people who want to get rich fall into temptation and a trap" (1 Tim. 6:6–10). To view work primarily as a way of getting rich rather than as a means to (1) minister, (2) gain autonomy, and (3) be able to help others who are in need, is to distort the nature of work.

What is your perspective about work? Do you evaluate your work merely in terms of what it offers you? Or do you evaluate your work in terms of what it enables you to do for others? God's perspective seems clear: work is ministry; work gives you and me opportunities to serve.